SpringerBriefs in Population Studies

Population Studies of Japan

The world population is expected to expand by 39.4 % to 9.6 billion in 2060 (UN World Population Prospects, revised 2010). Meanwhile, Japan is expected to see its population contract by nearly one-third to 86.7 million, and its proportion of the elderly (65 years of age and over) will account for no less than 39.9 % (National Institute of Population and Social Security Research in Japan, Population Projections for Japan 2012). Japan has entered the post-demographic transitional phase and will be the fastest shrinking country in the world, followed by former Eastern bloc nations, leading other Asian countries that are experiencing drastic changes.

A declining population that is rapidly aging impacts a country's economic growth, labor market, pensions, taxation, health care, and housing. The social structure and geographical distribution in the country will drastically change, and short-term as well as long-term solutions for economic and social consequences of this trend will be required.

This series aims to draw attention to Japan's entering the post-demographic transition phase and to present cutting-edge research in Japanese population studies. It will include compact monographs under the editorial supervision of the Population Association of Japan (PAJ).

The PAJ was established in 1948 and organizes researchers with a wide range of interests in population studies of Japan. The major fields are (1) population structure and aging; (2) migration, urbanization, and distribution; (3) fertility; (4) mortality and morbidity; (5) nuptiality, family, and households; (6) labor force and unemployment; (7) population projection and population policy (including family planning); and (8) historical demography. Since 1978, the PAJ has been publishing the academic journal *Jinkogaku Kenkyu* (The Journal of Population Studies), in which most of the articles are written in Japanese.

Thus, the scope of this series spans the entire field of population issues in Japan, impacts on socioeconomic change, and implications for policy measures. It includes population aging, fertility and family formation, household structures, population health, mortality, human geography and regional population, and comparative studies with other countries.

This series will be of great interest to a wide range of researchers in other countries confronting a post-demographic transition stage, demographers, population geographers, sociologists, economists, political scientists, health researchers, and practitioners across a broad spectrum of social sciences.

More information about this series at http://www.springer.com/series/13101

James M. Raymo · Miho Iwasawa

Diverging Destinies

The Japanese Case

Springer

James M. Raymo
Department of Sociology
University of Wisconsin-Madison
Madison, WI
USA

Miho Iwasawa
National Institute of Population and Social Security Research
Chiyoda-ku, Tokyo
Japan

ISSN 2211-3215 ISSN 2211-3223 (electronic)
SpringerBriefs in Population Studies
ISSN 2198-2724 ISSN 2198-2732 (electronic)
Population Studies of Japan
ISBN 978-981-10-0184-0 ISBN 978-981-10-0185-7 (eBook)
DOI 10.1007/978-981-10-0185-7

Library of Congress Control Number: 2016945780

Printed on acid-free paper

This Springer imprint is published by Springer Nature
The registered company is Springer Science+Business Media Singapore Pte Ltd.

Contents

Chapter 1
"Diverging Destinies": A Review of the Research

1.1 Introduction

"Diverging destinies" is a term used by Sara McLanahan in her 2004 presidential address to the Population Association of America to describe growing socioeconomic differentials in family behaviors associated with the second demographic transition. Drawing primarily on evidence from the U.S., McLanahan (2004) demonstrated that women at the lower end of the socioeconomic spectrum are increasingly engaging in family behaviors that are associated with reduction in the resources available to their children (e.g., nonmarital childbearing) while those at the upper end of the spectrum are engaging in family behaviors associated with increased resources (e.g., stable marriage). The core of her argument is that this pattern of family bifurcation has important implications for inequality in opportunities for success across generations. Because McLanahan explicitly linked this pattern of diverging destinies to the broader constellation of family changes associated second demographic transition, it is useful to begin with a brief overview of research on those changes.[1]

The "second demographic transition" is a framework for understanding the emergence of below-replacement fertility in industrialized countries and the accompanying changes in family behavior and related attitudes (Lesthaeghe 2010; van de Kaa 1987). Family changes associated with the second demographic transition include delayed marriage, delayed childbearing, increases in the proportion who never marry and remain childless, and substantial increases in nonmarital cohabitation, nonmarital fertility (including fertility within cohabiting unions),

[1]It is important to note that there is disagreement about not only the concept of a second demographic transition, but also about the idea of diverging destinies being part of the second demographic transition. Noting the role played by highly educated innovators in conventional depictions of family change associated with the second demographic transition, growing socioeconomic differences in family behavior have also been referred to as a "pattern of disadvantage" (e.g., Perelli-Harris et al. 2010; Perelli-Harris and Gerber 2011).

J.M. Raymo and M. Iwasawa, *Diverging Destinies*,
Population Studies of Japan, DOI 10.1007/978-981-10-0185-7_1

maternal employment, and divorce (Lesthaeghe 1995; Lesthaeghe and Moors 2000; van de Kaa 1987). This "package" of new family behaviors has emerged, with variations in both the timing and the magnitude of change, across nearly all low-fertility countries (Lesthaeghe and Moors 2000; Sobotka 2008). Explanations for family changes associated with the second demographic transition include shifting attitudes and values, convergence in men's and women's roles in society and within families, and improvements in contraceptive technology. Interested readers can consult several broad overviews of the second demographic transition (Lesthaeghe 1995, 2010; Raymo 2015a; Sobotka 2008; van de Kaa 1987, 2001).

Like research on the second demographic transition, the growing body of work on diverging destinies seeks to evaluate the generality of socioeconomic bifurcation in family behavior and to understand the ways in which the pace and nature of these changes are shaped by the social, economic, and political context in which they are observed (e.g., Perelli-Harris et al. 2010; McLanahan and Jacobsen 2015; Raymo et al. 2015). Our goal in this study is to extend this research by focusing on Japan—a relatively understudied country in which educational differences in family behavior appear to be growing despite many reasons to believe that a pattern of diverging destinies is unlikely to emerge. We accomplish this goal in three steps. In this first chapter, we set the stage by describing the pattern of diverging destinies in greater detail, summarizing its posited causes and consequences, and evaluating related empirical evidence from the U.S. and other low-fertility countries. In the second chapter, we turn our attention to Japan—discussing the theoretical value of extending research on diverging destinies to the Japanese context and providing an overview of the relatively small body of research on trends in educational differences in family outcomes based on Japanese data. In Chaps. 3 and 4, we use data from multiple rounds of the Japanese National Fertility Survey to describe trends over time in educational differences in a wide range of family outcomes. The goal of these analyses is to provide a comprehensive and systematic summary of empirical evidence that can provide a basis for evaluating the extent to which patterns of family change in Japan are consistent those emphasized in discussions of diverging destinies.

1.2 "Diverging Destinies" as Part of the Second Demographic Transition

The concept of diverging destinies emerges from a large body of research documenting growing socioeconomic differentials in family behavior over the past 30–40 years in the U.S. Family scholars have repeatedly demonstrated that men and women at the lower end of the socioeconomic spectrum are increasingly engaging in family behavior that differs from that of their counterparts at the upper end of the spectrum (see Cherlin 2010 for a summary of this research). Bifurcation in family behavior includes an increasing concentration of union formation and childbearing at relatively young ages, childbearing that occurs outside of marriage or cohabiting unions, and unintended fertility among men and women with lower levels of educational attainment (Ellwood and Jencks 2004; England et al. 2012; Kennedy and Bumpass 2010; Musick et al. 2009; Upchurch et al. 2002). In addition to early (often unplanned) family formation, lower education is also now associated with a higher likelihood of never marrying in the U.S. (Goldstein and Kenney 2011). Within families, highly educated mothers are more likely to be stably employed across the life course (McLanahan and Jacobsen 2015). Marital dissolution is another example of differential change, with evidence of stable or declining divorce rates among highly educated couples and increasingly fragile unions, and associated growth in multi-partner fertility, among the less educated (Cherlin 2009; Martin 2006; Raley and Bumpass 2003; Tach et al. 2011). Most of the research on diverging destinies has focused on growing differences between women with a four-year college degree or more and women who completed high school or less education, but attention is also increasingly being paid to "moderately-educated" Americans (those who have completed some college). Several studies show that men and women in this group are increasingly moving away from their counterparts with a college degree and more closely resembling those with less education (Cherlin 2011; McLanahan and Jacobsen 2015).

A good deal of research on low-SES families in the U.S. focuses on the distinctive features of "fragile families." These are families formed as a result of nonmarital childbearing and characterized by subsequent instability in parental relationships and family structure (Kalil and Ryan 2010; Osborne and McLanahan 2007). Births to unmarried mothers are common in the U.S., with 36 % of children born to unmarried mothers in 2013. The prevalence of such families differs markedly by race (29 % for whites vs. 68 % for blacks) and by educational attainment (57 % for those who did not complete high school vs. 9 % for those with a college degree) (Shattuck and Kreider 2013). Many of the important contributions to this research are based on data from the *Fragile Families and Child Well-being Study*—a multisite study of a large sample of births to urban mothers in 1998–2000. By following children and their mothers from birth through age nine, these data have allowed researchers to describe family experiences across the socioeconomic spectrum.

While efforts to document growing family differentials are most prominent in the U.S., a similar pattern of change is visible in many low-fertility societies. The claim that socioeconomic bifurcation is a universal feature of family change associated with the second demographic transition was made initially, and perhaps most compellingly, by McLanahan (2004) who used data from the Luxembourg Income Study (LIS) to show that young mothers, single mothers, and nonemployed mothers are more prevalent at lower levels of education in the U.S., Canada, and several Western European countries. The results of other cross-national analyses of educational differences in family behavior are generally consistent with the claim that diverging destinies is not a uniquely American phenomenon. Several studies provide evidence of growing socioeconomic differences in union formation (Kalmijn 2013; Raymo et al. 2015; Rendall et al. 2010), childbearing within cohabiting unions (Perelli-Harris et al. 2010), family structure (Heuveline and Weinshenker 2008), female labor force participation (Steider et al. 2016), and union dissolution (Härkönen and Dronkers 2006; Matysiak et al. 2014). We describe this cross-national evidence in greater detail below.

This empirical evidence of widespread socioeconomic bifurcation in family behavior is compelling given strong reasons to expect that patterns of family change should be shaped by context. For example, we might expect limited family bifurcation in societies characterized by low levels of economic inequality, given the strong reciprocal linkages between family behavior and aggregate levels of inequality (McLanahan and Percheski 2008). Similarly, we might expect to see less family bifurcation in relatively gender-inegalitarian settings where women's life course outcomes are not strongly shaped by their own educational attainment and where the family life course has been relatively homogeneous (Kalmijn 2013). The fact that we see growing socioeconomic differentials in union dissolution in countries with low levels of income inequality like Sweden (e.g., Kennedy and Thomson 2010) is compelling evidence of the broad relevance of family bifurcation. The fact that existing research on diverging destinies has paid relatively little attention to countries where gender roles remain highly asymmetric and the family life course has been characterized by little variation (Brinton 1992) makes our focus on Japan a potentially important source of contextual insight. We develop these ideas in greater detail toward the end of this chapter.

1.3 Implications of Differential Family Change

The potential implications of growing socioeconomic differences in family behavior are profound. Because family behaviors concentrated at lower levels of education tend to be associated with less favorable economic, social, and health outcomes, whereas those concentrated at higher levels tend to be associated with better outcomes, a key concern is how differential patterns of family change reproduce social and economic advantage or disadvantage across generations.

We begin by focusing on potential implications at the individual level. Recognizing that many of the family behaviors examined in the diverging destinies literature are directly or indirectly associated with children's exposure to single-parent families (e.g., nonmarital childbearing, divorce, early childbearing, unintended childbearing), we use this section to summarize research related to the implications of growing up in a single-parent family. This is a common experience in the U.S., where the proportion of children living with an unpartnered parent reached 25 % in 2012 (Vespa et al. 2013). Most importantly for our discussion of diverging destinies, it is also clear that the prevalence of single-parent family structure is concentrated at the lower end of the educational distribution (Vespa et al. 2013).

In their landmark study, McLanahan and Sandefur (1994) used multiple data sources to demonstrate that children of single mothers fare less well on a range of educational, behavioral, and economic outcomes. Their findings have been corroborated by a large number of studies showing that children from single-mother families complete less education (Powell and Parcel 1997), earn less (Biblarz and Raftery 1993), and exhibit more behavioral problems, including aggression, early childbearing (Wu and Martinson 1993), and delinquency (Matsueda and Heimer 1987). Related research finds that children of divorce have lower average levels of psychological well-being, as measured by happiness, life satisfaction, depression, and anxiety (Amato and Sobolewski 2001; Biblarz and Gottainer 2000; Cherlin et al. 1998; Osborne and McLanahan 2007; Ross and Mirowsky 1999). Children born to unpartnered mothers or to cohabiting mothers are more likely to experience greater family instability (McLanahan 2009; Musick and Michelmore 2015; Osborne et al. 2007) and several studies demonstrate that family instability is associated with less favorable outcomes for children (Cavanagh and Huston 2006; Osborne and McLanahan 2007; Fomby and Cherlin 2007; Wu 1996). It is also clear that instability is much higher among less-educated mothers (Musick and Michelmore 2015). Similar to instability, multi-partner fertility, and the formation of complex families are more prevalent among less-educated parents and are negatively associated with the well-being of both mothers and their children (Carlson and Furstenberg 2006; Manning et al. 2010; Osborne and Ankrum 2015; Waldfogel et al. 2010).

Research on how single-parenthood and related family behaviors contribute to growing differences in children's resources focuses on the financial, temporal, health, and social resources available to children in different family circumstances. Union dissolution, or family instability more generally, is a well-established correlate of women's economic well-being (Aassve et al. 2007; Avellar and Smock 2005; Meadows et al. 2008; Smock et al. 1999) and research on single parenthood and children's outcomes has repeatedly demonstrated the primary importance of economic resources (Carlson and Corcoran 2001; McLanahan and Sandefur 1994; Smith et al. 1997). The importance of economic resources reflects access to better schools and safer neighborhoods, parents' emotional well-being and parenting quality, and investment in children's educational development and recreation activities (e.g., Duncan and Brooks-Gunn 1997; Duncan et al. 1998; Thomson et al. 1994). It appears that the relevance of relationships between parents' economic resources and children's outcomes is increasing in the U.S. Parents in all socioeconomic strata are spending more money on children than in the past, but the gap between highly educated and less-educated parents' financial investment in children is growing (Lundberg and Pollack 2013).

The transition to single parenthood often entails changes in parenting (Astone and McLanahan 1991; Thomson et al. 1992) that are detrimental to the well-being of children (Amato 2005; Mclanahan and Sandefur 1994; Thomson et al. 1994). Without the economic contributions of a spouse or cohabiting partner, the limited earnings potential of many single mothers often results in economic hardship and necessitates relatively long work hours (Kalil and Ryan 2010; Sigle-Rushton and McLanahan 2002). Economic hardship is associated with less effective parenting (Conger et al. 1992) while long work hours limit the time available for children and contribute to emotional strain that is thought to result in less-engaged and inconsistent parenting (Jackson et al. 2000; Milkie et al. 2004). Several studies show that single mothers have worse emotional and physical health and higher levels of parenting stress relative to their married counterparts (Cooper et al. 2009; McLanahan 2009). Differences in parenting quality may also reflect more direct, shorter term increases in maternal depression following divorce (Amato 2000; Meadows et al. 2008) or the selection into single-parent families of mothers whose personality traits or stressful life experiences make them less effective parents (e.g., Amato 2005). Importantly, the link between relationship transitions and compromised parenting quality appears to be stronger for less-educated mothers (Beck et al. 2008; Cooper et al. 2009). Thus less-educated mothers are not only more likely to experience relationship transitions, but their parenting quality is also more negatively impacted by these transitions.

A large body of closely related research examines how union status is associated with parents' (typically mothers') well-being. This work shows that single parenthood is associated with less favorable outcomes for mothers as well, including higher levels of poverty, greater psychological distress, and worse physical health (Amato and James 2010; Brady and Burroway 2012; Johnson and Wu 2002; Meadows et al. 2007, 2008). Single parenthood is also associated with greater residential instability, which has negative implications for both neighborhood resources and access to support (Harknett and Knab 2007).

Research on the aggregate-level implications of family bifurcation focuses on assessing the extent to which the rise in single-parent families in the U.S. and the increasing concentration of these families at the lower end of the socioeconomic spectrum have contributed to the observed growth in social and economic inequality (Ellwood and Jencks 2004; Esping-Andersen 2007; Gottschalk and Danziger 2005; Martin 2006; Western et al. 2008) and declining intergenerational mobility (Beller 2009; Biblarz et al. 1997; Tach 2015). The results of this research are mixed and depend on the time period, the method of analysis, and measure of inequality or well-being considered (McLanahan and Percheski 2008). For example, Martin (2006) finds that the growing prevalence of families headed by never-married mothers has contributed significantly to the rise in income inequality in the U.S. whereas Western et al. (2008) find that rising inequality within groups is much more important than changes in family structure.

In addition to the role of nonmarital fertility, union dissolution, and family instability more generally, stratification researchers are increasingly focusing on increasing educational assortative mating. Although patterns of spouse pairing are not part of McLanahan's (2004) focus, it is clear that marriages in the U.S. are increasingly likely to be educationally homogamous at both ends of the educational distribution (Schwartz and Mare 2005). More marriages involving highly educated men and women, combined with greater marital stability at the top of the educational distribution, stronger labor force attachment of highly educated mothers, and growing returns to college education have resulted in an increasing concentration of "power couples" at the high end of the household income distribution (Greenwood et al. 2014). Combined with increased family instability and stagnating wages at the lower end of the educational distribution, patterns of assortative mating and the associated increase in the resemblance of spouses' earnings have played a significant role in the rise in income inequality in the U.S. (Schwartz 2010).

Some scholars have stressed the importance of the reciprocal, reinforcing nature of relationships between family behavior and inequality. Not only do changes in family behavior, especially the rise in single-parent families, contribute to increase in income inequality, but higher income inequality is also associated with lower marriage rates (Gould and Paserman 2003) and higher divorce rates (Burstein 2007). These aggregate-level relationships are thought to reflect inequality in men's capacity to meet the economic "bar" for marriage and to fulfill the role of stable provider within marriage (McLanahan and Percheski 2008). In the U.S., these relationships also play an important role in reinforcing racial and ethnic inequalities given the correlation between race and socioeconomic status (education) and large racial differences in family behavior (e.g., Elwood and Jencks 2004; McLanahan and Percheski 2008; Ventura and Bachrach 2000).

1.4 Posited Explanations

A wide range of explanations has been offered for growing socioeconomic differentiation in family behavior. McLanahan (2004) put forth the following four interrelated explanations: (a) the development of feminism, (b) the spread of new birth control technologies, (c) changing labor market conditions and associated changes in attitudes regarding men's and women's economic roles in the family, and (d) changes in welfare policies. To our knowledge, subsequent research has not systematically examined the first two factors so our summary of these explanations will draw primarily on McLanahan's own writing. Research on the roles of changing labor market conditions, attitudes, and public policies is plentiful so we are able to provide a broader discussion of these factors. For each of these posited explanations for change, it is important to consider how those at the higher and lower ends of the educational distribution have been impacted differently.

With respect to feminism, the basic claim is that shifting attitudes toward men's and women's work and family roles have provided women with new identities other than wife and mother. McLanahan (2004) argues that not only have opportunities to invest in careers and the development of identities outside of the family been more plentiful for highly educated women, but highly educated men have also been more supportive of women's push for more gender-egalitarian marriages. Among highly educated women, growing incentives to invest in careers are thought to lead to later marriage and childbearing, increased access to higher paying, more rewarding work is thought to contribute to more stable labor force attachment, and increasingly egalitarian marriages are thought to contribute to greater family stability. As McLanahan and Jacobsen (2015) argue, this resembles the more general emphasis on ideational change as part of the second demographic transition. The difference is that the impact of ideational change may depend on gender context, with highly educated "elites" choosing stable marriage as a preferred context for self-actualization in settings characterized by greater gender equality (Kalmijn 2013). Importantly for emphases on diverging destinies, there is reason to believe that part of this self-actualization among the highly educated involves leveraging marriage to facilitate intensive parental investment in children's success (Lundberg and Pollack 2013). Consistent with these changes, there is some evidence of increasing differences in attitudes toward family and divorce, with less-educated women becoming relatively more permissive in their attitudes toward divorce (Martin and Parashar 2006).

New birth control technologies (primarily the pill and legalized abortion) have contributed to growing family differentials in two ways. Women's ability to control their fertility has allowed those with higher educational and career aspirations to delay pregnancy and parenthood while investing in human capital and perhaps extending their search for a well-matched partner (Oppenheimer 1988). For women at the lower end of the educational spectrum, changes in birth control technology have contributed to more nonmarital childbearing by reducing expectations of marriage in response to unplanned pregnancy (Akerlof et al. 1996). Research on unplanned pregnancy and childbearing in the U.S. demonstrates a strong educational gradient. For example, Musick et al. (2009) find that, among white women, those with the lowest levels of education are three times more likely to have a mistimed birth and over six times more likely to have an unwanted birth relative to the most highly educated. They conclude that much of this difference may be explained by limited access to contraception, greater relationship instability, and lower levels of efficacy and self-regulation among women at the low end of the educational spectrum.

Changing labor market conditions of particular importance to the bifurcation of family behavior in the U.S. include the loss of stable, decent-paying low-skill jobs, and growth in "bad jobs" (especially for men with limited education) as well as increasing economic returns to higher education for men and especially for women (McLanahan 2004; McLanahan and Percheski 2008; Morris and Western 1999; Oppenheimer et al. 1997; Stevenson and Wolfers 2007). For women with low educational attainment, the combination of a limited pool of men upon whom they can rely economically and the perceived value of children as anchors in their own economically turbulent lives (Edin et al. 2004; Smock et al. 2005), has translated into a rise in nonmarital childbearing (often at relatively young ages). At the other end of the educational spectrum, women's increasing employment and economic resources appear to facilitate both marriage and marital stability (Schoen et al. 2006; Sweeney 2002; Sweeney and Cancian 2004).

These changes in the economic returns to education, combined with convergence in expectations regarding men's and women's economic roles within marriage (Cherlin 2009; Lundberg and Pollack 2013; Sweeney 2002) suggest that highly educated women's earnings and economic contributions increase the likelihood of marriage (albeit at later ages) and reduce the risk of marital dissolution (Oppenheimer 1997; Stevenson and Wolfers 2007). Stated differently, changes in labor market conditions and the relative opportunities available to men and women have reduced the benefits associated with the pooling of complementary specializations within marriage (Becker 1981) while increasing the benefits of assortative mating with respect to earnings potential (Oppenheimer 1988, 1997; Schwartz 2010). The increasing tendency for marriages to be homogamous with respect to both educational attainment and earnings (Schwartz 2010; Schwartz and Mare 2005) is consistent with this pattern of change. Although McLanahan's original articulation of the diverging destinies thesis did not directly address patterns of assortative mating, these trends are consistent with growing differentials in the resources available to children.

The changes in public policies most relevant to discussions of diverging destinies are those that limit public income support or welfare. Of particular importance is the shift from family policies characterized by universal benefits to programs characterized lower levels of benefits and greater means-testing. The argument is that universalistic, family-friendly public policies facilitate marriage across the educational spectrum and help to stabilize marriages among couples with the most limited earnings potential (Härkönen and Dronkers 2006). In contrast, less generous, means-tested programs provide particularly strong incentives for highly educated women to delay marriage and childbearing while investing in human capital that will facilitate entry into marriage (in light of increasing symmetry in men's and women's expected economic contributions to marriage) and subsequent marital stability (e.g., McLanahan and Jacobsen 2015; Rendall et al. 2009). For women with the weakest earnings capacity, who are also most likely to partner with men in similarly precarious economic circumstances, limited public support reduces the disincentives to early childbearing, often outside of marriage or a stable partnership. This interpretation is consistent with evidence of expanding educational differences in family behavior following welfare reforms of the mid-1990s in the U.S. and with evidence that educational differences in family outcomes associated with diverging destinies are more pronounced in societies characterized by less generous family policy regimes (Rendall et al. 2009; Schulze and Tyrell 2002).

1.5 Generality and Variation Across Time and Space

Discussions of "diverging destinies" are similar to research on the broader patterns of family change comprising the second demographic transition in recognizing that cross-national differences in the pace and magnitude of family bifurcation may reflect differences in policy, demography, or social context. Scholars have focused on (a) evaluating the extent to which the general pattern of family bifurcation highlighted by McLanahan (2004) is observed across countries, (b) identifying family behaviors and countries for which the general pattern does not appear to hold, and (c) attempting to identify contextual factors that contribute to observed cross-national differences in the degree of bifurcation (and its change over time).

A number of cross-national studies have examined change over time in educational differences in family behavior. This work has examined the educational gradient in marriage timing and patterns of union formation (Kalmijn 2013; Perelli-Harris and Amos-Lyons 2014; Rendall et al. 2003, 2005, 2009, 2010), union dissolution (Härkönen and Dronkers 2006; Kalmijn 2013; Matysiak et al. 2014), childbearing among unpartnered women (Perelli-Harris et al. 2010), and early childbearing (Raymo et al. 2015). The results of these studies generally demonstrate a pattern of bifurcation in family behaviors. For example, Perelli-Harris and colleagues (2010) find that childbearing within cohabitation is more common at lower levels of educational attainment across Europe and Raymo and colleagues (2015) show that the negative educational gradient in early childbearing has become stronger over time in many countries and has become weaker in none.

In addition to these multi-country studies, a good deal of research has examined educational gradients in family behavior and their change over time in specific countries. Examples include documentation of the emergence or strengthening of a negative educational gradient in divorce in Korea (Park and Raymo 2013), the Netherlands (De Graaf and Kalmijn 2006), Sweden (Hoem 1997), and the U.K. (Chan and Halpin 2005), research showing an increase in the association between low education of mothers and children's experience of parental separation in Sweden (Kennedy and Thomson 2010), and evidence of an emerging negative educational gradient in the likelihood of never marrying in the U.S. (Goldstein and Kenney 2001). McLanahan and Jacobsen's (2015) summary of this research concludes that findings are generally consistent with the claim that growing differentials in family behavior are a universal characteristic of low-fertility countries.

However, it is certainly not the case that all findings are consistent with a pattern of diverging destinies. In some cases, the educational gradient in family behaviors associated with reduced resources is positive. For example, divorce is more common among highly educated women in Italy and other southern European countries (Härkönen and Dronkers 2006). In other cases, educational differences in family behavior are small (Matysiak et al. 2013) or are explained by country-level factors (Perelli-Harris and Amos-Lyons 2014). Finally, there are other studies that document a strong educational gradient in the family behavior of interest but find little evidence of change over time in educational differences. For example, Raymo et al. (2015) found no evidence of statistically meaningful change in the negative educational gradient in early childbirth in ten of the twenty countries they examined. Overall, existing empirical evidence is generally consistent with the pattern described by McLanahan (2004), but there is also an abundance of evidence pointing to the need for caution in evaluating the generality of a pattern of diverging destinies. Much of this cautionary evidence highlights the importance of contextual factors in shaping socioeconomic differences in family behavior and their change over time.

Our own reading of the cross-national evidence suggests the importance of four contextual factors. First, it seems safe to say that the U.S. is an extreme case, with educational divergence in family behavior much more pronounced than in most other countries. For example, Perelli-Harris and Amos-Lyons' (2014) examination of educational differences in partnership trajectories across 14 countries found that the U.S. fits nicely with the expectations of "diverging destinies"—with trajectories characterized by union dissolution and long-term cohabitation concentrated at lower levels of education—but evidence for other countries is more mixed. Similarly, Carlson et al. (2014) found that the negative educational gradient in children's exposure to unpartnered-parent family structure is far more pronounced in the U.S. than in the other 14 countries they studied. In addition to evidence that the U.S. is somewhat of an outlier, cross-national studies point to the importance of differences in public policy, the level of economic inequality, and the degree of gender inequality in shaping cross-national differences in pace and nature of socioeconomic bifurcation in family behavior.

The role of public policy is suggested by McLanahan's (2004) focus on increasing means-testing and reductions in levels of public income support as an explanation for family bifurcation in the U.S. The argument is that educational differentials (and growth therein) should be less pronounced in countries with a strong public safety net because more generous, universal welfare policies reduce differences across educational categories in the costs or benefits associated with engaging in specific family behaviors. Broad support for this posited relationship can be found in a series of papers in which Rendall and colleagues examine socioeconomic differences in the timing of childbearing in a number of European countries (Rendall et al. 2003, 2005, 2009, 2010). Their analyses show an increasing concentration of relatively early childbearing among women with lower levels of education and occupational status in countries with less generous, means-tested welfare policies (i.e., English-speaking countries and Southern Europe) but declining educational differentials in age at first birth in countries with more generous, universal welfare policies (Northern and Western Europe). Similarly, the multilevel models estimated by Härkönen and Dronkers (2006) show that welfare generosity is associated with a smaller educational gradient in divorce.

Another contextual factor that appears to be related to the degree of family bifurcation is the degree of economic inequality. As noted above, the reciprocal linkages between inequality and family bifurcation have been emphasized in research on the U.S. (McLanahan and Percheski 2008). Here, the argument is that high levels of income inequality make it difficult for those at the bottom of the socioeconomic distribution to generate and maintain the economic resources necessary for marriage and for marital stability. Consistent with this emphasis, Kalmijn (2013) finds that measures of educational inequality (educational differences in unemployment and poverty) are associated with a stronger negative educational gradient in marital dissolution for men (but not for women).

One of the most intriguing findings from the cross-national research summarized above is that the negative educational gradient in family behaviors associated with reduced resources is stronger in more gender-inegalitarian countries. As discussed in the next chapter, this is a central focus in our expectations regarding educational differences in family behavior in Japan. Here, the basic argument is that policies or social structures facilitating work–family balance reduce the opportunity costs of family transitions that compete with employment (e.g., early childbearing, single parenthood). Stated differently, the greater the difficulty that women face in working while raising children, the more likely women with the highest earnings potential will be to engage in family behaviors that facilitate continued employment (e.g., delayed marriage, delayed childbearing, marriage to high-earning men, stable marriage). Evidence consistent with this emphasis includes relatively weak educational gradients in Northern European countries and stronger educational gradients in relatively gender-inegalitarian countries in Southern Europe (e.g., Perelli-Harris et al. 2010; Rendall et al. 2010). More direct evidence comes from multilevel models that include country-specific indicators of gender equality or support for work–family balance. For example, Kalmijn (2013) finds that highly educated women are more likely to be married and less likely to be divorced in more gender-egalitarian countries.

Most of the cross-national research on educational differences in family behavior is limited by its lack of attention to differences across countries in the nature and meaning of various family outcomes. For example, analyses of childbearing within cohabitation (e.g., Perelli-Harris et al. 2010) and analyses of patterns of union formation (e.g., Perelli-Harris and Amos-Lyons 2014) are complicated by the fact that the duration, nature, and selectivity of cohabiting unions are qualitatively different across countries. In the U.S., nonmarital childbearing is often to unpartnered mothers or to mothers in relatively unstable partnerships whereas most unmarried mothers in western and northern European countries are in stable, marriage-like cohabiting unions (Heuveline and Timberlake 2004; Kiernan 2001). Similarly, efforts to understand cross-national differences in early childbearing (Raymo et al. 2015; Rendall et al. 2009, 2010) are complicated by the fact that the meaning of "early" varies across both time and space. While these studies do make reference to these issues, it is not easy to incorporate such contextual specificity within a comparative analytical framework. One insight from this work is that the prevalence of a given family behavior may be a good predictor of the direction and strength of the educational gradient. When new behaviors (i.e., those associated with the second demographic transition) are relatively uncommon, they are more likely to be experienced by "innovators" who tend to be more highly educated. As the formerly nonnormative behavior becomes more common and the social and economic costs of engaging in the behavior decline, other factors such as those listed above become more relevant and the positive gradient diminishes, disappears, and ultimately a negative gradient appears. This general argument has been made in several studies (Härkönen and Dronkers 2006; Matysiak et al. 2014; Park and Raymo 2013; Raymo et al. 2015).

1.6 Summary

McLanahan's (2004) paper on "diverging destinies" is one of the most widely cited publications in family demography, but related research has focused almost exclusively on the U.S. and Western Europe. This relatively narrow geographical focus is an important limitation. Comparable evidence from low-fertility countries in other parts of the world is required to evaluate the claim that increasing socioeconomic differences in early childbearing observed in the U.S. and Western Europe are indeed a universal feature of family change associated with the second demographic transition. Perhaps more importantly, evidence from countries characterized by very different social, economic, and political contexts can provide insights into the ways in which the pace and the nature of family change associated with diverging destinies depend upon context. For a variety of reasons, Japan is a particularly informative case to evaluate the generality of patterns observed in the U.S. and other western countries and to develop contextual modifications to the notion of diverging destinies.

As noted at the beginning of this chapter, there are good theoretical and empirical reasons to believe that the pattern of family bifurcation associated with diverging destinies is unlikely to emerge in Japan. At the same time, there are good reasons to believe that such change may be underway. As described in the next chapter, Japan is a country that has long been characterized by relatively low levels of socioeconomic inequality and a homogenous and highly scripted family life course (Brinton 1992). Importantly, Japan is also perhaps the most gender-inegalitarian wealthy country. To the extent that theoretical emphases on feminism and growing gender symmetry in work and family roles have contributed to observed patterns of family bifurcation, similar change is unlikely in Japan. The contraceptive environment in Japan also contrasts with theoretical explanations for observed patterns of family change in the U.S. and elsewhere.

Strong theoretical reasons to expect similar patterns of family bifurcation in Japan include the policy environment and changing labor market conditions. Public expenditures on family support are relatively low and the weak public policy support of work–family balance in Japan is well documented (Schoppa 2006; Yu 2009). Combined with rapid improvements in educational attainment for women and large economic returns to higher education, this environment looks very similar to that thought to underlie the growing bifurcation in family behavior in the U.S. Also similar to the U.S. are growing income inequality (Ohtake 2005) and growing disparities in educational attainment and in the employment opportunities available to men and women. In the next chapter, we provide an overview of these changes, elaborate their potential implications for family bifurcation, and summarize empirical evidence of growing educational differences in several aspects of family behavior.

Another more fundamental argument against the potential for growing family bifurcation might be that Japan is not actually experiencing the second demographic transition, so there is thus little reason to expect a pattern of diverging destinies. However, this argument makes sense only if one takes a rather narrow view of the second demographic transition and if one views a pattern of family bifurcation as something that is conditional on the second demographic transition. In our view, neither of these stances are particularly helpful—there are no universally accepted criteria for what constitutes a second demographic transition country and there is no strong reason to expect that the pattern of diverging destinies described above depends on all features of the second demographic transition (however defined) being present. Furthermore, there is also disagreement about whether observed patterns of family bifurcation should be incorporated within the second demographic transition or treated as an alternative framework for understanding family change (Perelli-Harris et al. 2010). As we discuss in the next chapter, focusing on countries like Japan is valuable precisely because of this theoretical ambiguity.

Chapter 2
The Japanese Context and Existing Empirical Evidence

2.1 Introduction

To evaluate claims that empirical patterns based largely on data from a single country are broadly generalizable, two types of comparative research are useful. One involves gathering data from a large number of countries and comparing patterns across those countries. This can involve descriptive analysis (McLanahan 2004; McLanahan and Jacobsen 2015; Perelli-Harris et al. 2010; Raymo et al. 2015; Rendall 2010) or multilevel regression analysis (Härkönen and Dronkers 2006; Kalmijn 2013). This approach is powerful for its ability to describe or estimate relationships between the outcome of interest and contextual variables of theoretical relevance. The second type involves focusing on a single country (or small number of countries) characterized by distinctive features of theoretical interest, such as specific policies and distinctive social or cultural factors (e.g., Rendall et al. 2009). This approach is powerful for its ability to provide detailed insights into the specific conditions under which the general pattern of interest does or does not hold. In both cases, the key source of information is theoretically relevant contextual similarities or differences across countries.

Japan is rarely included in large cross-national studies of educational differences in family behavior (see Carlson et al. 2014; Raymo et al. 2015 for exceptions), but several studies have examined socioeconomic differentials in family behavior within the country (e.g., Fukuda 2013; Ono 2003; Raymo 2003). In contrast to the U.S. (and to a lesser degree, European countries), research on Japan that explicitly addresses the notion of diverging destinies is very limited. Indeed, a recent search of Google Scholar found only two Japanese language research papers that reference McLanahan's (2004) paper. This limited attention to diverging destinies may reflect a view among Japanese social scientists that family change in Japan does not really fit into the larger second demographic transition framework. A few studies have addressed the question of whether Japan is experiencing a second demographic transition (e.g., Atoh et al. 2004; Matsuo 2001), but very low levels of nonmarital

J.M. Raymo and M. Iwasawa, *Diverging Destinies*,
Population Studies of Japan, DOI 10.1007/978-981-10-0185-7_2

childbearing, the relatively low prevalence of cohabiting unions (Atoh 2001a), and limited evidence of "individuation" in attitudinal data (Atoh 2001b) may limit the perceived relevance of the second demographic transition framework and related questions regarding diverging destinies. As noted in the previous chapter, we view McLanahan's (2004) explicit linkage of diverging destinies with the second demographic transition as suggestive, but not necessarily implying that family bifurcation will occur in tandem with the progression of family changes typically associated with the second demographic transition. Our goal in this chapter is to provide an overview of both empirical and theoretical reasons to expect that family change in Japan may, or may not, be consistent with the patterns in research on diverging destinies or the "pattern of disadvantage" described in the previous chapter.

To accomplish this goal, we draw heavily upon our own work. Over the past decade, we have published several studies that articulate key reasons to believe that Japan is an unlikely setting for changes that conform to a pattern of diverging destinies. These include the long history of homogeneity in the family life course, limited use of modern contraception, and perhaps most importantly, a relatively strong maintenance of highly asymmetric work and family roles for husbands and wives. At the same time, our past research has recognized several features of the Japanese context that are potentially consistent with the kind of family bifurcation observed in the U.S. and many other low-fertility settings. Chief among these are relatively limited public spending on families and a rapidly changing employment environment that has had a very different impact on those at the upper and lower ends of the educational distribution, with implications for social and economic inequality.

2.2 Reasons not to Expect a Pattern of Diverging Destinies in Japan

2.2.1 Homogenous Family Life Course

One compelling reason to expect limited socioeconomic divergence in family behavior is history. The family life course in Japan has long been distinguished by its homogeneity (Brinton 1992), with the timing and ordering of family transitions following a well-established script with relatively little variation. Earlier changes in the timing of marriage and childbearing and in the level of fertility occurred similarly across the socioeconomic distribution (Hodge and Ogawa 1991; Raymo 2003), reflecting both structural forces and normative constraints on women's opportunities outside of the family (Brinton 1992, 1993). Women's own expectations about their work and family trajectories are also consistent with a socioeconomically homogenous life course (Raymo et al. 2015b). This lack of educational variation suggests that differentials in new family behaviors that do emerge in Japan may be less pronounced than in the U.S. and Europe. At the same time, evidence that being a full-time housewife is less of a "status symbol" than it was (Kohara 2007) and that there are large educational differences in women's ideal work–family trajectory (Raymo et al. 2015b) suggest that the foundations of this family homogeneity may be shifting, at least with respect to mothers' employment.

2.2.2 *Contraceptive Environment*

Japan's distinctive contraceptive environment is another reason to expect limited socioeconomic differentials in family change—especially in patterns of family formation. The range of contraceptives used in Japan continues to be limited primarily to condoms, rhythm, and withdrawal (Sato and Iwasawa 2006). All of these are cheap (or free), but all have high failure rates relative to the irreversible and hormonal methods more commonly practiced in the U.S. and most other low-fertility countries (Kost et al. 2008). There are some educational differences in self-reports of contraceptive use and abortion, with women at the lower end of the educational spectrum less likely than women with tertiary education to use contraception at last intercourse and more likely to report having had an abortion (Raymo et al. 2015b). However, Japan's distinctive contraceptive environment has not changed much over time (Sato and Iwasawa 2006) and there is little reason to expect that socioeconomic differences in contraceptive access or efficacy should contribute to differences in patterns of pregnancy and union formation.

Abortion is also widely available and not so expensive as to limit access among women with lower levels of education and more limited economic resources. Survey data show that 20–25 % of women in all education groups (except those who did not complete high school) said that they would abort a pregnancy resulting from contraceptive failure (Raymo et al. 2015b). Abortion is readily available and its relatively low cost is unlikely to be a barrier to women wishing to terminate unplanned pregnancies. In conjunction with the reliance on cheap, accessible contraception, this easy access to abortion suggests that educational differences in early childbearing and nonmarital childbearing should be limited in Japan.

2.2.3 *Gender Division of Labor*

Gender equality figures prominently in efforts to understand cross-national differences in marriage and fertility (McDonald 2000a, b, 2009) but has received less attention in research on socioeconomic differences in family behavior. However, there are theoretical and empirical reasons to expect that gender context plays a role in shaping the pace and nature of family bifurcation, with differentials less pronounced (or perhaps reversed) in more inegalitarian societies (e.g., Kalmijn 2013). This pattern is clear in studies of divorce, with divorce among highly educated women more common in relatively inegalitarian southern European countries (Härkönen and Dronkers 2006; Kalmijn 2013).

This focus may be particularly important for understanding patterns of family change in Japan, one of the most gender-inegalitarian wealthy countries. The 2014 Global Gender Gap Index (World Economic Forum 2014) ranks Japan 104th out of 142 countries, primarily reflecting the large gender wage gap and limited representation of women in management and in politics. Perhaps more important for understanding patterns of family behavior is the division of labor within the family. OECD data on time use show that Japan has one of the largest gender gaps in time spent in unpaid labor (housework, childcare, and other family care). Japanese women spend 4.8 times as much time on these tasks as men, with only Korea having a higher ratio (5.1 times) (http://www.oecd.org/gender/data/balancingpaidworkunpaidworkandleisure.htm, accessed on January 4, 2016). To the extent that this highly asymmetric division of household labor is not strongly related to socioeconomic status, we would expect that divorce, cohabitation, nonmarital fertility, and other family behaviors associated with lower resources for children would, if anything, be more prevalent among highly educated women for whom the opportunity costs of entering a conventional breadwinner-homemaker marriage would be highest (Kalmijn 2013). However, it may be that a positive correlation between socioeconomic status and more egalitarian division of household labor contributes to differentials more consistent with a pattern of diverging destinies. Tsuya et al. (2005) show that the husbands of more highly educated women do more housework and that this relationship has become stronger over time, suggesting the possibility of growing educational differences in divorce, women's labor force participation, and other related family outcomes.

2.3 Reasons to Expect a Pattern of Diverging Destinies in Japan

2.3.1 Public Policy

Public policies related to families in Japan are generally consistent with those thought to contribute to growing bifurcation in family outcomes. Levels of public support for families are generally low and benefits are typically means-tested. Japan has one of the lowest levels of spending on social policies among wealthy countries. Japan spends less than 2 % of GDP on family benefits, which is well below the OECD average and about half the level of countries with the highest family expenditures (OECD 2015). Welfare benefits (*seikatsu hogo*) are relatively limited and conditions for qualification are stringent. Despite recent growth in the number of welfare recipients, the number of recipients in households with children has remained stable (Ohtake et al. 2013). This is one reason why, as discussed below, a relatively high proportion of single mothers are in poverty despite working full time and often living with parents. Because many poor families do not qualify for welfare benefits, public income support is limited to a small universal child allowance (*kodomo teate*) and somewhat larger means-tested childrearing allowance (*jidō fuyō teate*) (about $500 per child) for single parents (Abe and Ōishi 2005; Akaishi 2011; Raymo and Zhou 2012). These benefits have become more restrictive in recent years (Abe and Ōishi 2005) and Japan's welfare policy environment can be seen as similar in some ways to that associated with bifurcation in family behavior in the U.S. (McLanahan 2004).

For women with higher levels of education—who have higher earnings capacity themselves and are more likely to be married to higher earning husbands—the opportunity costs of divorce and single motherhood are thus high. Similarly, the opportunity costs of early family formation (which may prevent both investment in her own human capital and the search for spouse with high earnings) may be particularly high for highly educated women given limited support for childrearing and strong tax incentives for married women to limit their own earnings in order to maintain dependent exemption on their husband's taxes (Akabayashi 2006). Limited support for childrearing includes insufficient access to high-quality, affordable day care (especially in large metropolitan areas), and expectations of long work hours and long commutes (Boling 2007; Yamaguchi 2005). Recognizing that this policy environment may be contributing to Japan's very low fertility rate, recent policy efforts have sought to improve women's ability to balance full-time employment and family responsibilities. These efforts include the expansion of parental leave following birth, increase in the level of salary replacement during leave, the option to work shorter hours, and other support for private sector efforts to facilitate work–family balance (Nagase 2014). These policy initiatives should work to limit socioeconomic differences in family behavior by reducing the opportunity costs of early childbearing, divorce, and single parenthood and by facilitating continuous attachment to the labor force across the socioeconomic spectrum. However, existing empirical evidence casts doubt on the effectiveness of these efforts. While it is true that there has been a substantial increase in the proportion of women who take maternity leave, there is little evidence of change in the proportion of women who exit the labor force following childbirth. In other words, more women are taking childcare leave before exiting the labor the force than in the past, but the total proportion leaving has remained stable (Nagase and Moriizumi 2013; National Institute of Population and Social Security Research 2012). Educational differences in post-birth labor force attachment have, to our knowledge, not yet been studied. We provide some of the first evidence on this question in Chap. 4.

2.3.2 *Changing Employment Environment*

Perhaps the most compelling reason to expect patterns of family bifurcation similar to those observed in the U.S. and elsewhere is major change in the Japanese labor market. Three particularly important and interrelated trends are the rapid spread of nonstandard employment, wage stagnation, and increasing returns to higher education for women. During Japan's "lost 20 years" following the end of the "bubble economy" in 1989, the unemployment rate increased and the prevalence of nonstandard employment has grown markedly among both men and women (Brinton 2011; Osawa et al. 2013; Shire 2002). Importantly, both of these trends have been most pronounced at lower levels of education and in young adulthood (Kosugi 2004), when men and women are finishing their education, entering the labor market, entering the marriage market, and starting to think about parenthood. Nonstandard work typically does not pay well, provides little or no security, and rarely provides benefits (Osawa et al. 2013) and early exposure to these jobs has lasting implications for economic well-being across the life course (Genda et al. 2010; Sakai and Higuchi 2005; Yu 2012). Some studies have examined how unemployment and exposure to "bad jobs" are related to marriage and fertility (Kondo 2014; Nagase 2002; Ogura and Kadoda 2008; Piotrowski et al. 2015; Raymo and Shibata 2014), but we are not aware of any research that has explicitly considered the ways in which these labor market changes are associated with educational differences in family outcomes.

As in other countries, stagnating or declining real wages, especially for men with lower levels of education, mean that it is increasingly important for both spouses to work and contribute to the family economy (Oppenheimer 1997). As discussed in the previous chapter, the increasing symmetry in men's and women's economic contributions to the family has implications for family outcomes central to the diverging destinies literature. Perhaps most important are the implications for marriage timing, non-marriage, and assortative mating. Increasing valuation of women's earnings potential in the marriage market means that highly educated women will marry later, but be more likely to ever marry (Goldstein and Kenney 2001; Oppenheimer 1988) and more likely to marry highly educated men (Schwartz and Mare 2005). Because preferences for female educational hypergamy and the breadwinner-homemaker model of marriage are deeply entrenched in Japanese society (Kohara 2007; Raymo and Iwasawa 2005), these changes would represent a major shift in family behavior. Evidence that these changes have occured differently across the educational distribution (as in the U.S.) would have important implications for inequality and processes of stratification within and across generations.

2.3.3 Growing Inequality

Despite widespread interest in growing economic inequality and rising levels of poverty in Japan, very little attention has been paid to the role of differential family change (see Sudo et al. 2012 for an exception). Japan has long been viewed as a relatively egalitarian country (Moriguchi and Saez 2008), but has become somewhat more unequal since the 1980s, with the Gini coefficient for household disposable income rising from 0.30 in 1985 to 0.34 in 2009 (OECD 2016a). Growth in poverty is also pronounced, with the proportion of the population living in relative poverty (equivalized household income less than half of the national median), rising from 0.12 to 0.16 over the same period (OECD 2016a). As discussed in the previous chapter, economic inequality is intricately linked with family behavior in the U.S. (McLanahan and Percheski 2008) and cross-national studies have found that higher levels of inequality are associated with a stronger negative educational gradient in divorce (Härkönen and Dronkers 2006). Our analyses cannot shed light on the complex relationships between inequality and family behavior, but existing research on the U.S. and elsewhere suggests that the rising levels of inequality and poverty make Japan ripe for growing socioeconomic bifurcation in family behavior. We now turn our attention to existing research on educational differences in the family outcomes linked to diverging destinies.

2.3.4 *Trends in Educational Attainment*

Trends in educational attainment are closely related to trends in inequality. In the not so distant past, relatively few women attended university as this was considered unnecessary and even detrimental to marriage prospects (Brinton 1993). Because the proportion of men and women completing high school has long been over 90 %, the scarcity of female university graduates meant that most women stopped their formal education following high school or junior college, neither of which provided women with career orientation or the kind of human capital rewarded in the labor market. In this context, there was arguably little variation either employment aspirations or the opportunity costs associated with early family formation. Similarly, there may have been little socioeconomic variation in the social stigma associated with unconventional family behaviors.

Figure 2.1 shows that the proportion of women entering four-year universities increased rapidly from the mid-1980s. Nearly half of female high school graduates now enter a four-year university, a figure that is only slightly lower than that for

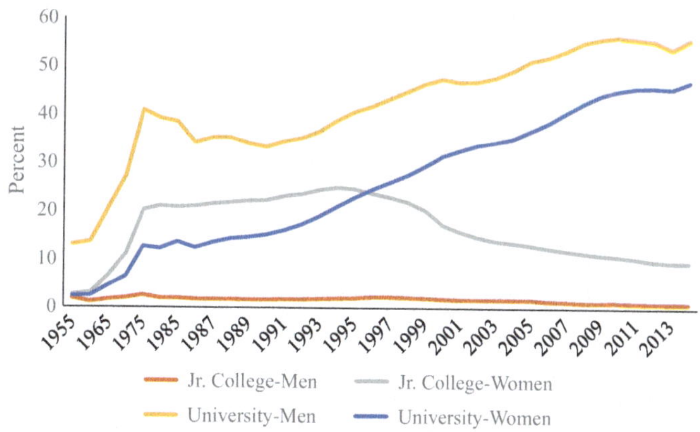

Fig. 2.1 Rates of continuation to tertiary education, by college type and sex. *Source* NIPSSR (2016), citing data from Gakkō Kihon Chōsa (Basic Education Survey)

men. As the proportion attending junior college rapidly shrinks, women are increasingly concentrated at the high and low ends of the educational spectrum (university graduates and high school or vocational school graduates). To the extent that these groups differ with respect to life orientation, employment opportunities, perceived work–family tradeoffs, support from partners/husbands, or the perceived costs of violating social norms, we might expect them to follow increasingly different family pathways, as in the U.S. and other countries discussed in the context of diverging destinies.

2.4 Empirical Evidence

In the remainder of this chapter, we briefly describe what is known about educational differences in family behavior and how those differences have changed over time. We focus first on aspects of union formation and dissolution, then on aspects of childbearing, and finally on patterns of maternal labor force participation.

2.4.1 Union Formation and Dissolution

2.4.1.1 Marriage Timing

At first glance, research on marriage timing and the probability of ever marrying suggests that the pattern of diverging destinies observed in the U.S. and elsewhere is of little relevance in Japan. Research on marriages taking place in the 1970s and 1980s consistently found that women with higher educational attainment and higher earnings married later and were less likely to ever marry than their lower SES counterparts (Ono 2003; Raymo 2003; Tsuya and Mason 1995). This pattern is less consistent with diverging destinies than it is of a more "traditional" scenario in which women's economic contributions to marriage were limited and in which men, even those at the lower end of the socioeconomic spectrum, were capable of supporting a family as the primary breadwinner. In this context, higher education enabled women to achieve a degree of economic independence that allowed some to postpone or opt out of the "the onerous status of the Japanese wife and mother" (Tsuya and Mason 1995: 156).

However, more recent research on marriages in the 1990s and 2000s suggests that this pattern is changing in ways that may be consistent with the general picture painted in the diverging destinies literature. For example, Fukuda (2013) finds that, in contrast to Ono's (2003) results, earnings are positively associated with the transition to marriage among women born in the 1970s. Similarly, Fukuda and Raymo (2015) find that the negative educational gradient in women's marriage has disappeared among recent cohorts. This reflects both the relatively high marriage rates of college-educated women beyond age 30 in recent years and the declining rates of marriage among women with less than a four-year degree in the late 1990s and beyond. In closely related research on employment status and marriage, several studies have found that men and women in nonstandard employment (a group that includes large proportions of the less educated) are less likely to marry than those in regular employment (Nagase 2002; Piotrowski et al. 2015). These patterns are suggestive of the growing economic difficulties of maintaining a breadwinner-homemaker marriage. Attitudinal data support this interpretation, with both husbands and wives indicating that they would like wives to work more hours than they currently do (Bumpass et al. 2010) and unmarried men indicating an increased preference for marriages in which their wives are employed (NIPSSR 2012: 62). In Sect. 3.3, we provided updated evidence on change over time in the educational gradient in marriage—focusing on the likelihood of early marriage. To what degree do we see an increasing concentration of early marriage among women at the lower end of the educational spectrum, as predicted by research on diverging destinies?

2.4.1.2 Educational Assortative Mating

Japan has long been characterized by a high degree of educational assortative mating (Suzuki 1991; Watanabe and Kondo 1990; Yasuda 1971). The strong tendency for educational homogamy or female hypergamy is clearly important for understanding educational differences in marriage behavior in response to rapid relative improvements in women's educational attainment. For example, Raymo and Iwasawa (2005) showed that the increased competition for a relatively smaller pool of highly educated men contributed to the decline in marriage rates among highly educated women during the period 1980–1995.

Patterns of diverging destinies suggest that the tendency for homogamous pairings should be increasing at both the top and the bottom of the educational distributions. Consistent with this, Ishida and Motegi (2014) show that the likelihood of educational homogamy is much higher among four-year college graduates and those with a high school degree or less than it is among those in the middle category (vocational school and junior college). Recent research on trends in assortative mating is limited, but there is some evidence that educational homogamy is, if anything, declining (Raymo and Xie 2000; Smits and Park 2009). For example, Fukuda and Raymo (2015) find that the propensity for highly educated women to marry men with less education than themselves has increased in recent years (see also Iwasawa 2013). They speculate that this reflects women's response to the marriage market mismatch described by Raymo and Iwasawa (2005) as well as shifting attitudes among men regarding wives' relative educational attainment and economic contributions to the family. They do not find any evidence of an increase in the propensity for educational homogamy among those with a high school education or less, suggesting that trends in educational assortative mating in

Japan are not consistent with a growing bifurcation of resources at the two ends of the socioeconomic spectrum as observed in the U.S. (Schwartz 2010). In Sect. 3.4, we will provide updated figures on patterns of educational assortative mating.

2.4.1.3 Cohabitation

Research on nonmarital cohabitation in Japan is limited and we know little about educational differences in the prevalence and nature of cohabiting unions. It is clear that cohabitation has increased markedly in recent years and that experience of cohabitation is somewhat more common at the lower end of the educational distribution (Iwasawa 2006; Raymo et al. 2009; Tsuya 2006). It is also clear that cohabiting unions are less likely than marriages to be educationally homogamous (Ishida and Motegi 2014). It is less clear, however, whether trends in cohabitation (and its relationship to marriage) conform to patterns emphasized in research on diverging destinies. Of particular interest in that research is the bifurcation of cohabitation into a precursor to marriage among more highly educated men and women and an alternative to marriage among those with lower levels of education. Relative to their more highly educated counterparts, women with lower levels of education in the U.S. are increasingly having children in relatively unstable non-marital unions (Kennedy and Bumpass 2008). So, even if cohabitation is now widespread in the U.S., the meaning of these unions varies across the educational spectrum in ways that have differences for the resources available to women and their children.

There is little evidence with which to evaluate the relevance of this scenario in the Japanese context. Raymo et al. (2009) showed that cohabitation is rarely an alternative to marriage, but that cohabitation among the less educated more often involves transition to marriage following pregnancy. To the extent that these pregnancies are unplanned (Raymo et al. 2015b), and to the extent that marriages precipitated by unplanned pregnancies (within cohabiting unions) are more likely to subsequently dissolve, this pattern is potentially consistent with growing bifurcation in family resources. We explore this possibility more directly in Sect. 3.5.

2.4.1.4 Divorce

Divorce has risen markedly over the past 25 years in Japan, with as many as one in three marriages projected to end in divorce (Raymo et al. 2004). Evidence regarding educational differences in divorce is mixed and is subject to important data limitations, including substantial underreporting of divorce in sample surveys (Raymo 2008). Seeking to avoid the limitations of existing survey data, an earlier study by Raymo et al. (2004) used census data and indirect estimation methods to show that educational differences in the prevalence of divorced individuals were minimal in the 1980 but increased markedly through 2000. By 2000, women with a high school degree, and especially those who did not complete high school, were substantially more likely to have divorced relative to women completed at least some tertiary education.

Other studies have found a negative educational gradient in divorce, especially for men (Katō 2005; Ono 2009), but these studies did not consider change over time in the educational gradient. Raymo (2008) used two different sources of data to conclude that divorce is negatively associated with women's educational attainment, but he found no evidence of change over time in the educational gradient. Similar results were found in the most recent and most comprehensive study to date on trends in educational differences in divorce. Raymo et al. (2013) used two different sources of data to show that women who completed some tertiary education were 30–50 % less likely to divorce in a given year than high school graduates, but they found no evidence that this differential has changed over time. Importantly, they also found that the strong negative educational gradient in divorce remained statistically significant after controlling for a range of posited economic and family correlates. Speculative interpretation of these findings suggested the potential importance of factors such as differential selection into marriage in a setting where a large proportion of men and women are projected to never marry and educational differences in the meaning of marriage, especially with respect to the role of marriage as a mechanism for intensive investment in children (see Lundberg and Pollack 2013 for related ideas regarding educational differences in marriage in the U.S.). Consistent with earlier studies, Raymo et al. (2015b) also demonstrated that women who did not complete high school have a much higher risk of divorce than women in any other educational group. Although this is a very small and increasingly select group, they appear to be disadvantaged in many ways and we will include them in our examination of recent trends in divorce in Sect. 3.6.

2.4.1.5 Single-Mother Families

The rise in divorce rates has resulted in a substantial increase in the prevalence of single-parent families and the strong negative educational gradient in divorce means that many of these families are headed by women with a high school education or less. One recent study showed that 54 % of single mothers have a high school education or less, compared to 41 % of married mothers (Raymo 2015b). We are unaware of any research on change over time in the educational composition of single mothers, but the evidence of little change in the educational gradient in divorce just summarized suggests that the degree of concentration of single parenthood among the less educated has likely remained stable. Evidence that educational differences in remarriage are small and have not changed over time

(Raymo and Iwasawa 2014) is also consistent with stability in the educational composition of single mothers.

A growing body of research on the well-being of single mothers provides a wealth of evidence directly relevant to the idea of diverging destinies. Much of this work is based on the National Survey of Households with Children conducted by the Japan Institute for Labour Policy and Training (Zhou 2014). While this work does not focus explicitly on the role of single motherhood in contributing to socioeconomic differences in children's resources, it does demonstrate the many disadvantages faced by these families. The fact that single mothers are heavily concentrated among the less educated provides indirect evidence of diverging destinies as a salient feature of the Japanese family landscape.

While nearly 90 % of single mothers are employed, over half of single-mother households live below the poverty line (OECD 2016b). Economic disadvantage is thus a defining feature of single-mother families and is only partially mitigated by the common strategy of "doubling up." As shown by Shirahase and Raymo (2014), about one-third of single mothers coreside with their parents but, in many cases, these older parents are also economically disadvantaged. Other research has shown that, relative to married mothers, single mothers report lower levels of self-rated health and emotional well-being (Raymo and Zhou 2012; Raymo 2015b), spend less time with their children (Raymo et al. 2014), and report that their children have more health problems and perform less well in school (Raymo 2016). To a large degree, these disadvantages are explained by the relatively high levels of economic deprivation among single-mother families. These results are consistent with compelling qualitative evidence of the difficulties faced by single mothers and their children (Abe 2008) and suggest that divorce and single parenthood is a particularly relevant mechanism for the intergenerational transmission of disadvantage as suggested by research on diverging destinies. Because the National Fertility Survey does not provide sufficient information to consistently identify single mothers across time, we do not include analyses of this outcome in Chap. 3.

2.4.2 *Childbearing*

2.4.2.1 Age at First Birth

While much of the research on the second demographic transition focuses on delayed childbearing and the extent to which women are "catching up" at older ages, a primary concern of research on diverging destinies is about the increasing concentration of early childbearing, typically outside of marriage and often outside of stable unions, among less-educated women. As noted in the previous chapter, this focus is motivated by the large body of research demonstrating that this pattern of family formation is negatively associated with the subsequent well-being of both children and mothers. In contrast to the U.S., early childbearing is uncommon in Japan. In 2010, only 1 % of all births were registered to teenage mothers and only 10 % were registered to women age 20–24 (National Institute of Population and Social Security Research 2015).[1]

Nevertheless, it is clear that these early births are concentrated among at the lower end of the educational spectrum. For example, Raymo et al. (2015b) show that nearly all teenage births are to women who failed to complete high school and that about one-fourth of first births to women with a high school education or less occur in the early 20s, compared to only 6 % among university graduates. They also show that the relatively high prevalence of unintended first births among less-educated mothers is partially explained by this relatively high prevalence of early births. Research on trends in educational differences in early childbearing in Japan is limited, but a recent study by Raymo et al. (2015b) finds little evidence of change across cohorts in the concentration of early childbearing among women with a high school education or less. We provide updated evidence on early childbearing in Sect. 4.2.

2.4.2.2 Nonmarital Childbearing

In contrast to low-fertility societies in the West, the prevalence of nonmarital childbearing has remained negligible in Japan. The proportion of all births registered to unmarried mothers reached 2 % in 2005 after hovering around 1 % since the 1960s (National Institute for Population and Social Security Research 2015). Because the prevalence of nonmarital childbearing is so low, research on this pathway to family formation is limited. It is clear, however, that nonmarital births are much more common among women with lower levels of education. Tabulations presented by Raymo et al. (2015b) show that among first births occurring between 1995 and 2005, the proportion to unmarried mothers was 5 % for those who did not complete high school and vocational school graduates, 3 % among high school graduates, and only 1 % among four-year college graduates.

Despite the low levels of nonmarital childbearing, it is clear that relationships between pregnancy and marriage have changed markedly. This is most evident in the sharp rise in bridal pregnancy (marriages preceded by pregnancy). The proportion of first marriages that was preceded by pregnancy doubled from 10 % in 1980 to 19 % in 2010 (Iwasawa and Kamata 2014). This pathway to family formation is heavily concentrated among women with lower levels of education and this negative educational gradient has increased sharply over time. Comparing the 1970s and 1990s marriage cohorts, Raymo and Iwasawa (2008) showed that the probability of first marriage preceded by pregnancy doubled for women with a high

[1]In the U.S., 6 % of births in 2015 were to teenage mothers and 21 % of births were to women age 20–24 (http://www.cdc.gov/nchs/data/nvsr/nvsr65/nvsr65_03.pdf, accessed June 3, 2016).

school education or less while remaining stable at significantly lower levels for women who completed a two- or four-year college degree.

One way to think about this trend is to view the emergence of pregnancy as a primary reason for marriage in a setting where other incentives to marry (especially at younger ages) have waned. That is, couples postpone marriage until pregnancy necessitates formalization of the relationship. The link between marriage and fertility remains strong, but the temporal ordering of marriage and pregnancy has reversed for many couples. This scenario would be consistent with the notion of diverging destinies if bridal pregnancies are associated with lower quality, less stable marriages. However, it would be less consistent if bridal pregnancies simply hasten stable marriages that would have occurred sooner or later. Carefully distinguishing between these two scenarios is an important task for future research.

The limited empirical evidence that is available appears more consistent with the first scenario. Raymo and Iwasawa (2008) found that the patterns of educational pairing in marriages preceded by pregnancy differ significantly from those not preceded by pregnancy, with women who are pregnant at the time of marriage much more likely to marry a man with less education than themselves. It is also clear that bridal pregnancies tend to be reported as unintended. Raymo et al. (2015b) find that the higher prevalence of unintended childbearing (among first births) for women with a high school education or less is partially explained by the fact that these women are more likely to have a first birth that was the result of a premarital pregnancy. Because female educational hypogamy and unintended childbearing have been linked to subsequent marital instability and lower levels of well-being, growing educational differences in the relationship between pregnancy and marriage may play an important role in the intergenerational transmission of disadvantage. We examine trends in educational differences in nonmarital childbearing and bridal pregnancy in Sects. 4.3 and 4.4.

2.4.2.3 Stepfamily Fertility

While the strong link between marriage and childbearing in Japan means that the growth in multi-partner fertility observed in the U.S. and Europe (Thomson et al. 2014) is limited, stepfamily fertility is potentially relevant. Evidence that about 40 % of divorced women remarry (Raymo and Iwasawa 2014) indicates the potential for rising levels of family complexity. However, the absence of research on remarriage means that we know very little about stepfamily fertility in Japan. There is some evidence that levels of childbearing within remarriages are quite low (Raymo and Iwasawa 2014), but nothing is known about educational differences in stepfamily fertility and their implications for family complexity and its role in shaping the intergenerational transmission of disadvantage. We summarize data on stepfamily fertility in Sect. 4.3.

2.4.2.4 Mother's Employment

As noted in Chap. 1, mothers' attachment to the labor force is another dimension of family change central to the pattern of diverging destinies. More stable employment in higher paying jobs for highly educated women is thought to contribute to growing family income inequality and bifurcation in the economic resources available to children (Schwartz 2010). The highly asymmetric division of labor within Japanese couples makes this a particularly interesting research focus. For women, higher education has long been associated with lower levels of employment because these women typically married high-earning men capable of supporting the socially desirable role of mother and homemaker (Brinton 1993; Kohara 2007). Recent research on socioeconomic differentials in married women's employment paints a mixed picture, with evidence of growth in dual-earner couples among those with the highest earnings potential (Kohara 2008) balanced by evidence that highly educated women are also the least likely to reenter the labor force after exiting prior to childbirth (Raymo and Lim 2011). In general, it appears that relatively high rates of labor force participation among less-educated women reflect economic necessity while the heterogeneous behavior of highly educated women reflects a split between those with preferences for career employment and those with preferences for a primarily domestic focus (Raymo and Lim 2011).

One potentially important dimension of stratification among mothers in the labor market is employment type. As in the U.S. and many other western countries, Japan has witnessed a rapid increase in nonstandard employment (Osawa et al. 2013; Rebick 2005). It is clear that this type of employment is heavily concentrated among women (Futagami 2010; Houseman and Osawa 2003), but less research has been done on educational differences in the type of employment. One recent study finds that nonstandard employment is more common among women with lower levels of education and links this pattern to educational differences in women's employment stability (Lim and Raymo 2014). Because women who reenter the labor market after exiting almost always work in nonstandard employment (Lim and Raymo 2014; Yu 2002), the instability of less-educated women's employment trajectory results in a higher prevalence of nonstandard employment. Married women with a four-year college degree are distinctive for the relative stability of their employment status (regardless of whether they are in standard employment, nonstandard employment, or not employed). Because nonstandard jobs tend to be low paid and provide little stability or opportunity for advancement, concentration of this type of employment among less-educated women is a potentially important mechanism of stratification consistent with ideas central to the notion of diverging destinies. We present data on the employment status of mothers in Sect. 4.5.

2.5 Synthesis of Existing Research

What does the existing evidence summarized above tell us about how Japan is similar and different to the U.S. and other Western societies? Is it consistent with the emergence of a pattern of diverging destinies in Japan? Our assessment is that the evidence is mixed and that the answers to these questions depend on the aspect of family change considered. Several of the family outcomes emphasized by McLanahan (2004) are indeed strongly differentiated by education in Japan. In particular, divorce, single parenthood, and a range of outcomes associated with early family formation are concentrated among women with lower levels of education. These include early childbearing, unintended fertility, bridal pregnancy, and nonmarital childbearing (albeit at very low levels). Evidence of an increase over time in these educational gradients is less convincing, however. In the following chapters, we therefore devote particular attention to describing trends in these educational gradients.

Educational differences in other family outcomes are less consistent with a pattern of diverging destinies. For example, there is little evidence that cohabitation is replacing marriage for less-educated women and no indication that cohabitation has emerged as a setting for childbearing for any educational group. Similarly, the continued high prevalence of labor force exit at childbirth across educational categories is not consistent with a scenario in which diverging employment trajectories for mothers is contributing to bifurcation in children's resources. In fact, evidence that the most highly educated women remain the most likely to permanently exit the labor force (Raymo and Lim 2011) is consistent with a more traditional view of the family in which women with the resources to do so choose to focus on domestic production.

After systematic empirical examination of the wide range of family behaviors discussed above, we will return to this question of the extent to which the diverging destinies framework is applicable to Japan. We will also consider possible explanations for observed similarities and differences between Japan and the more widely studied western countries. Our analyses will be primarily descriptive in nature and we are thus not able to directly evaluate the relevance of underlying mechanisms. Nevertheless, we can offer speculative interpretations that may provide a useful basis for subsequent research. Finally, we will evaluate what we have learned from our analyses (and the previous work summarized above) and consider the potential implications for stratification and intergenerational transmission of dis/advantage in the Japanese context.

Chapter 3
Union Formation and Dissolution

3.1 Introduction

In this chapter, we describe trends in educational differences for several dimensions of marriage and union formation—early marriage, nonmarital cohabitation, divorce, and husband's education. Before presenting these figures, we describe the data used for these analyses.

3.2 The National Fertility Survey

The National Fertility Survey (NFS) has been conducted by the National Institute of Population Problems and Social Security Research (Japanese Ministry of Health, Labour and Welfare) every five years since the second survey in 1952.[1] The analyses presented below are based on data from the 8th through the 14th surveys, conducted in 1982 and 2010, respectively. The NFS is a nationally representative survey of two populations: married women aged 18–49 and unmarried men and women aged 18–49.[2] The NFS is based on a two-stage systematic sampling of all census enumeration districts in Japan. More specifically, respondents are randomly selected from a systematic sample of between 325–840 census tracts drawn from the roughly 1000 tracts surveyed by the Kokumin Seikatsu Kisō Chōsa (Basic Survey of National Life, also conducted by the Ministry of Health, Labour and Welfare)

[1]The first survey was conducted in 1940. One exception to the five-year interval is the three-year interval between the 12th (2002) and 13th (2005) surveys, a change designed to align the NFS survey years with census years. The conducting institution changed its name from the Institute of Population Problems to the National Institute of Population Problems and Social Security Research in 1996.

[2]The 8th survey in 1982 was the first to sample unmarried men and women, motivating our focus on the 8th to the 14th surveys.

J.M. Raymo and M. Iwasawa, *Diverging Destinies*,
Population Studies of Japan, DOI 10.1007/978-981-10-0185-7_3

which were systematically sampled from the full population of census tracts established for the most temporally proximate national census. Questionnaires were distributed to all 18–49-year-old unmarried men and women and all 18–49-year-old married women residing in the sampled census tracts. The total sample size ranges from 13,346 in 1982 to 19,544 in 1992. The composition of the surveys with respect to marital status has changed over time as the trend toward later marriage has become more pronounced in Japan. In the 8th survey in 1982, 63 % of respondents were married women, but this proportion declined to 43 % in 14th survey in 2010. The response rates for both the married and unmarried samples have been consistently high. Not surprisingly, response rates have been higher among married women and response rates for both groups have declined over time. For married women, the response rate declined from 95 % in 1982 to 87 % in 2010 and the corresponding decline for unmarried women was from 86 % to 74 %. While the decline in response rates may be a cause for concern, it is important to note that these response rates are much higher than for most recent social surveys in Japan. For example, the response rate for the 2010 round of the Japan General Social Survey was only 62 %.[3]

The NFS is the best available source of data on family behavior over an extended period of time. Each survey contains information about the timing of women's current marriage, the timing of all births within the current marriage, information about cohabitation and divorce experience, information about husband's educational attainment, and information about women's employment following marriage and childbirth. More recent surveys include information about the duration of cohabiting unions and the timing of divorce and remarriage, but we are not able to use this information to examine trends in educational differences over long periods of time. The 8th–14th NFS samples include women born between 1932 and 1991, but we focus on women born between 1940 and 1979, splitting the sample into four ten-year birth cohorts. Exclusion of women born outside of this range reduces potential problems with small cohort size and allows us to focus on women who have had sufficient time to experience the events of interest.

Importantly, the NFS has collected consistent measures of women's educational attainment, allowing us to describe educational differences in family behavior and how those differences have changed over time. Educational attainment is measured with five categories representing the highest level of education completed at the time of the survey: junior high school, high school, vocational school, junior college, and university. The use of consistent categories is useful for making comparisons across time, but it is important to keep in mind the compositional shifts that have taken place with respect to educational attainment. Rising educational attainment means that university-educated women have become a less selective group over time while those who did not complete high school have become a more selective group. This compositional shift should be kept in mind when evaluating

[3]https://www.icpsr.umich.edu/icpsrweb/ICPSR/studies/34623 (accessed April 25, 2016).

change over time in educational differences in family behavior. In her work on diverging destinies, McLanahan (2004) and McLanahan and Jacobsen (2015) circumvented this problem by using reported years of education to construct a relative measure that reflects rising educational attainment (i.e., low, medium, and high education). Because the NFS only provides information on women's highest completed educational level, we are not able to implement a similar measurement strategy. Subsequent efforts to evaluate socioeconomic bifurcation in family behavior might profitably examine alternative specifications for the measure of socioeconomic status (SES) that are not plagued by this concern about cross-cohort comparability (due to changing patterns of educational selection).

The NFS includes data on both married and unmarried men, but we limit our focus to women for two important reasons. One is the fact that married men are not sampled directly. To examine men in the same way that we examine women would require us to construct records for married men based on the information provided by married women. This is problematic to the extent that the husbands of 18–49-year-old married women are not a representative sample of 18–49-year-old married men. A second reason is that most of the research on diverging destinies focuses on mothers, reflecting the centrality of nonmarital childbearing and single motherhood to our understanding of potential socioeconomic differences in children's access to resources.

In addition to the absence of direct responses from married men, the cross-sectional design and sampling frame of the NFS introduce some other potential limitations. For example, the NFS data contain no information on women who would have been sampled had they not died prior to the survey and women who were sampled but did not respond to the survey. Very low mortality suggests that the absence of information for the first group will be of little substantive importance, but nonresponse is likely to pose a more serious problem. Despite the consistently high response rates, differential nonresponse with respect to the variables of interest (especially educational attainment) would introduce a potentially important source of bias into the analyses summarized below.

3.3 Early Marriage

Much of the research on diverging destinies has focused on the growing concentration of early childbearing among women with lower levels of education. Because marriage and childbearing remain tightly linked in Japan, we examine trends over time in educational differences in the likelihood of marrying by age 22. This particular age is an admittedly arbitrary threshold, but it is relevant in that it corresponds to the age at which university graduates complete schooling and marriage before this age is relatively uncommon in Japan. According to census tabulations, the proportion of 22-year-old women who had ever married was 0.19 in 1980 and 0.09 in 2010.[4]

Because we employ a similar analytical strategy for most of the analyses presented below, we describe our approach in some detail here and note modifications in subsequent analyses. We begin by defining the outcome of interest as a 0–1 variable—marrying before one's 23rd birthday in this case. We then estimate a logistic regression model for this outcome as a function of women's age at the time of the survey, her educational attainment, her birth cohort, and the interaction between educational attainment and birth cohort. Because our interest is in the description of trends over time in educational differences, and not in evaluating explanations for those trends, we do not include any other covariates in the models. Based on results from this descriptive model, we calculate the predicted probabilities of marrying by age 22 for each combination of cohort and education. We then present these predicted probabilities graphically to provide both a visual and statistical representation of evidence to evaluate the emergence of diverging destinies. We restrict our analyses to women who were at least 23 years old when interviewed and present predicted probabilities for women age 30–34 when interviewed.

Figure 3.1 shows the predicted probability of marriage by age 22 across birth cohorts and educational attainment (here, and in subsequent figures, JHS refers to junior high school, HS refers to high school, VOC refers to vocational school, JC refers to junior college, and UNI refers to four-year college or more). At first glance, this figure suggests little support for a pattern of diverging destinies. The absolute difference between women with lower levels of education and those with higher levels was highest for the 1940s cohort and lowest for the 1970s cohort, reflecting the steady decline in early marriage for women of all educational levels except university graduates (for whom the probability has always been very low). A substantial proportion of women who did not complete high school continue to experience early marriage (35 % of the 1970s cohort married by age 22), but we believe it more informative to focus on comparisons of high school graduates with more highly educated women. As will be clear from subsequent figures, the small and increasingly select group of junior high school graduates are engaging in a much different pattern of family behavior than all other groups of women. This pattern is generally consistent with patterns of diverging destinies and merits attention, but we consider this group to be too small to serve as a meaningful comparison group.

Looking first at differences between high school graduates (our preferred reference group of less-educated women) and university graduates, we see that the *relative* difference has increased over time as the proportion in the latter group who experience marriage by age 22 has shrunk to nearly zero. The empty circle markers indicate that the difference between university graduates and high school graduates is statistically larger than in the first cohort (1940–49) and the solid circle marker

[4]http://www.e-stat.go.jp/SG1/estat/GL02100104.do?tocd=00200521 (accessed May 15, 2016).

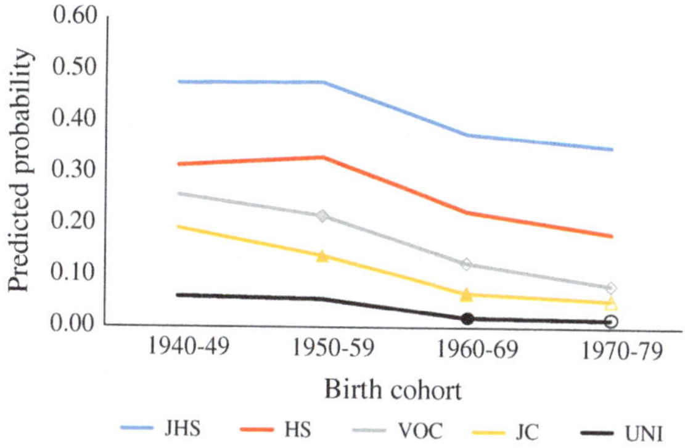

Fig. 3.1 Predicted probability of marriage by age 22, by education and birth cohort

indicates that the difference with high school graduates is larger than in both the first and the previous cohort.[5] The odds ratio for early marriage among university graduates relative to high school graduates declined from 0.14 in the earliest cohort to 0.07 in the 1960s and 1970s cohorts. So, while we do not see any obvious "fanning out" in the probability of early marriage for high school and university graduates, there is some evidence that the relative likelihood of early parenthood has grown across cohorts. This pattern is consistent with expectations articulated in the literature on diverging destinies.

An important focus in our analyses is on women in the two "intermediate" educational groups (vocational school graduates and junior college graduates). Motivated by the growing body of research documenting the increasing similarity of women with some college and high school graduates in the U.S., we are interested in assessing the extent to which vocational school and junior college graduates increasingly look more like women with less education or women with more education. We are also interested in assessing the extent to which these two groups increasingly differ from (or resemble) each other. This focus on the middle of the educational distribution will not only shed light on the relevance of patterns of diverging destinies in Japan, but will also provide insight into the nature of rapid shifts in women's educational outcomes. In particular, we are interested in assessing evidence of two plausible scenarios. In one, the rise in four-year education results in an increasingly selective group of women in the intermediate educational categories who increasingly look like their less-educated counterparts. This is what appears to be happening in the U.S. In another, the shrinking pool of junior college graduates consists of women with relatively strong family orientation whose family behavior resembles women with four-year degrees and increasingly differs from vocational school graduates whose family behavior more closely resembles high school

[5]There are few cases in which the difference is significantly larger than in the previous cohort but not larger than in the first cohort. We note those few cases and identify them with empty, dashed circles.

graduates. So, the second scenario is one in which family bifurcation is occurring among women with intermediate levels of education.

Figure 3.1 clearly shows a growing divergence between high school graduates and the two intermediate educational groups. In all cases, the difference in the predicted probability of early marriage for these groups (relative to high school graduates) is significantly larger than in the first cohort and this gap appears to be growing over time (although the change across cohorts is only statistically significant in one case). With respect to early marriage, these two groups increasingly resemble university graduates and continue to resemble each other. It is worth noting that change appears to be particularly pronounced for the 1960s birth cohort —growth in the gap with high school graduates was statistically different from zero in this cohort for both junior college and university graduates. That is, the difference in the probability of early marriage between these women and high school graduates was not only larger than in the 1940s birth cohort, but also larger than in the preceding (1950s) birth cohort. The odds ratio of early marriage for vocational school graduates relative to high school graduates declined from 0.75 in the 1940s cohort to 0.49 in the 1960s cohort. The corresponding decline for junior college graduates (relative to high school graduates) was from 0.52 to 0.25.

3.4 Husband's Educational Attainment

We estimated the predicted probability of marrying a man with a university degree across four different marriage cohorts (the 1960s, 1970s, 1980s, and 1990s). In addition to focusing on marriages during a particular time period or marriage cohort (rather than the experiences of a particular birth cohort), these models are different from those used in other analyses. Husband's characteristics have not typically been a focus of study in research on diverging destinies in the U.S., but we suspect that "match quality" is a strong predictor of children's resources in societies like Japan, where breadwinner-homemaker marriages remain common. Even if women are less like to be full-time homemakers, the continued prevalence of temporary labor force exit around childbirth results in highly gender-asymmetric economic contributions to household income. Educational attainment is strongly correlated with life-time earnings in most countries and Japan is no exception (Trostel et al. 2002). Earnings power remains a strong criterion in women's evaluation of potential spouses (Raymo and Iwasawa 2005) and it is clear that some family behaviors concentrated at lower levels of education (e.g., bridal pregnancy) are also associated with the "match quality" (Raymo and Iwasawa 2008). The increasing likelihood of homogamous marriages among highly educated men and women in the U.S. is thought to play a role in increasing income inequality and the intergenerational transmission of resources in the U.S. (Schwartz 2010; Schwartz and Mare 2005) and there is value in assessing the extent to which a similar pattern of change is observed in Japan.

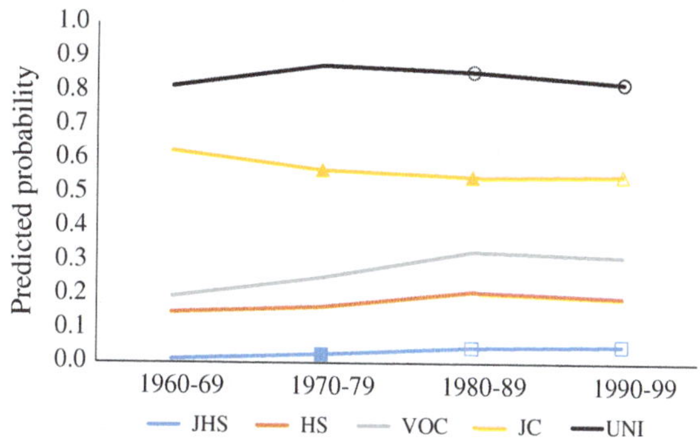

Fig. 3.2 Probability of marrying a university graduate by education and marriage cohort

Figure 3.2 presents the predicted probabilities of marrying a university-educated man, by marriage cohort (1960s, 1970s, 1980s, and 1990s). These figures reflect both trends over time in men's education (which should increase the probability of marrying a highly educated man) and pairing behavior. Contrary to expectations based on the diverging destinies framework, we see that the probability of marrying a highly educated man has increased for women with lower levels of education while remaining stable or declining for those with a university or junior college degree. The gap between university graduates and high school graduates is significantly smaller in the 1990s (relative to the 1960s), but the substantive change is not large (the size of the gap was 67 % points in the 1960s and 62 % points in the 1990s). More striking is the significant reduction in the gap between junior college and high school graduates, going from 48 % points in the 1960s to 36 % points in the 1990s. The very high likelihood of educational homogamy among university graduates is consistent with greater economic resources for the children of these couples, but there is little evidence to suggest a growing concentration of resources via assortative mating at the upper end of the educational distribution.

One shortcoming of the analyses summarized in Fig. 3.2 is that it is not possible to distinguish the extent to which observed trends reflect changing educational attainment (for both men and women) or changing patterns of spouse pairing, independent of changes in educational distributions. To address this limitation, we also estimated log-linear models for spouse pairing. Figure 3.3 presents estimates from models that account for change across ten-year marriage cohorts in the distribution of husbands' and wives' educational attainment. Because these models are based on tables of observed marriages, they do not account for change across cohorts in the likelihood of marriage (the same limitation characterizes the analyses summarized in Fig. 3.2). The results of these log-linear models are presented as odds ratios—the odds of marrying a university-educated man for women of a given education level, relative to the odds of educational homogamy for university-educated women. They are thus measures of the relative odds of marrying a highly educated man, net of men's and women's educational attainment.

Fig. 3.3 Odds ratio for marriage to a university graduate (relative to university graduates), by education and marriage cohort

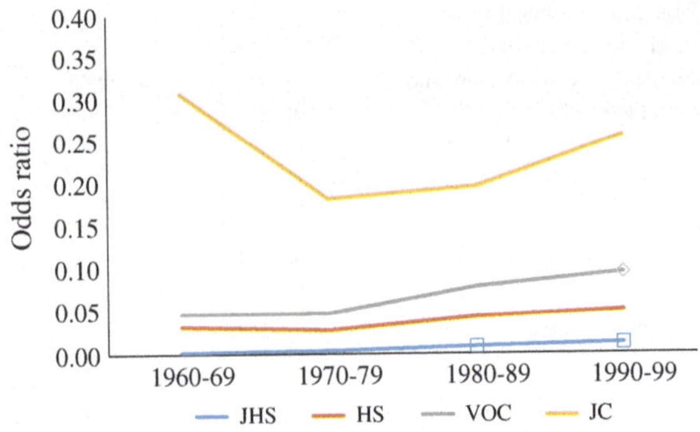

From this figure, we can see that the relative odds of marrying a university graduate are quite low for women with a vocational school education or less. However, similar to the results in Fig. 3.2, there is some evidence of an increase across marriage cohorts in the relative odds of marriages involving highly educated men and women with lower levels of education. We also see a sharp drop in the relative odds of marriage involving a woman with junior college education and a university-educated man in 1970s marriage cohort, followed by a slight rebound (but these changes are not statistically significant at $p < 0.05$). In sum, the likelihood that women with a vocational school degree or less marry a university-educated man remains relatively low, but there is no evidence of growing bifurcation with respect to who marries whom (at least with respect to these broad educational categories).

3.5 Cohabitation

As noted in Chap. 2, nonmarital cohabitation is an important family outcome in the diverging destinies literature to the extent that this arrangement is less stable than marriage and thus associated with more family transitions for children. This may be a less centrally relevant concern in Japan where childbearing within cohabiting unions is uncommon (Raymo et al. 2009), but cohabitation has been linked with other outcomes central to the diverging destinies literature, including bridal pregnancy (Raymo et al. 2009) and subsequent marital dissolution (Dush et al. 2003). Long-term trends in cohabitation are difficult to examine using the NFS data because information on nonmarital unions was not collected from currently married women before the 14th survey. The NFS also did not collect information on cohabitation duration until the 14th round, so we are quite limited in what we can say about educational differences in cohabitation. Nevertheless, we believe that, in light of the very limited body of empirical evidence on cohabitation in Japan, there is value in examining trends in cohabitation experience among currently unmarried women.

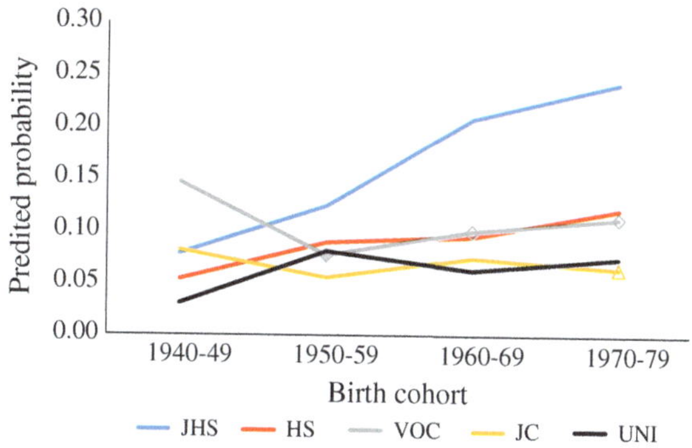

Fig. 3.4 Predicted probability of cohabitation experience, by education and birth cohort

Figure 3.4 presents the predicted probability that a currently unmarried woman has ever cohabited, by birth cohort and educational attainment. As with the analyses of early marriage, these results are based on a logistic regression model that includes the interaction between educational attainment and birth cohort and educational attainment. Three things are immediately clear from this figure. The first is that the absolute levels are very low—with a few exceptions, the predicted probability is at about 0.10 or less. The second is that there is some evidence of growth in cohabitation across cohorts. This pattern is consistent with that documented by Raymo et al. (2009), although the levels are much lower than in that study due to the fact that these NFS data do not include information on the cohabitation experience of currently married women. The third is that the trends in cohabitation for women with less than a high school education are much different than those for other women.

Looking at high school graduates in comparison to other groups, there is some visual evidence that the gap between these women and their counterparts with junior college and university degrees has grown over time. After converging in the 1950s birth cohort, high school graduates and vocational school graduates now look very similar. Differences between high school graduates and other groups are not large, but the difference with junior college graduates appears to have grown. The difference in the 1970s cohort is significantly larger than in the first cohort (1940s). The predicted probability of cohabitation among unmarried university graduates is now very similar to that of junior college graduates, but differences between high school graduates and university graduates are not statistically significant.

3.6 Divorce

Like cohabitation, the information on divorce available in the NFS is not ideal. Because exposure to the risk of divorce commences at marriage, analyses of divorce require information on both the date of marriage and the date of divorce (if applicable). However, prior to the 13th round, the only information collected on

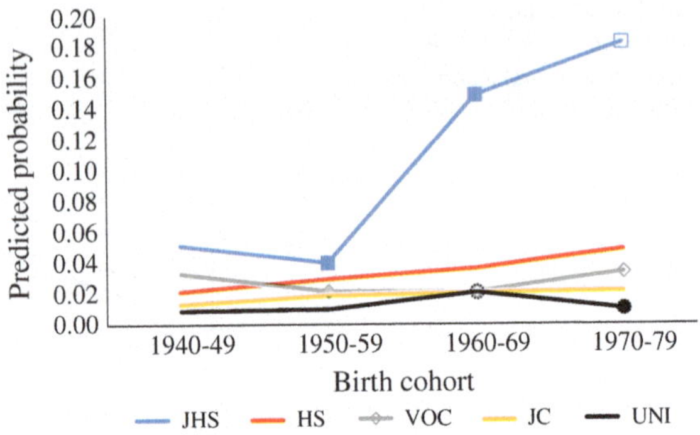

Fig. 3.5 Predicted probability of divorce experience, by education and birth cohort

divorce in the NFS was whether or not a woman had ever experienced divorce.[6] Our analyses of longer term trends are therefore limited to whether or not women reported ever experiencing divorce.

Figure 3.5 shows results from logistic regression models of divorce experience as a function of the covariates described above. Here, the analytical sample is restricted to women who had ever married and the results presented are the predicted probability that a 30–34-year-old women reported that she had divorced. The most notable feature of the figure is the rapid rise in divorce among the least-educated women, consistent with predictions of diverging destinies for this group. Very high levels of divorce among women who did not finish high school have been documented by Raymo et al. (2013), among others. The level of divorce in Fig. 3.5 is very low (probabilities are below 0.05 for most combinations of educational attainment and birth cohort), reflecting the fact that the predicted probabilities are for 30–34-year-old women, many of whom have only been at the risk of divorce for a short period of time. It is also possible that low levels of divorce reflect underreporting of divorce experience in the NFS, as noted by Raymo (2008) and Raymo et al. (2013). There is some evidence of growing differences between high school graduates and more highly educated women in recent birth cohorts. This is particularly true of the difference between high school graduates and university graduates born in the 1970s (the solid black circle for this group indicates that the difference between university and high school graduates is significantly larger than in both the first (1940s) cohort and the most recent (1960s) cohort). While this evidence of family bifurcation is much less pronounced than that documented in the U.S. (Martin 2006), it is nonetheless suggestive of growing differences in marital stability at either end of the educational distribution.

The results in Fig. 3.5 describe trends in a limited measure of divorce experience over a long period of time, but are not ideal in that they also reflect changes in marriage timing. The trend toward later age at marriage means that 30–34-year-old

[6]Questionnaires for the 8th and 14th round of NFS did not distinguish divorce from widowhood, but we do not view this as particularly problematic given the very low levels of mortality prior to age 50 (the age of the oldest women in the NFS).

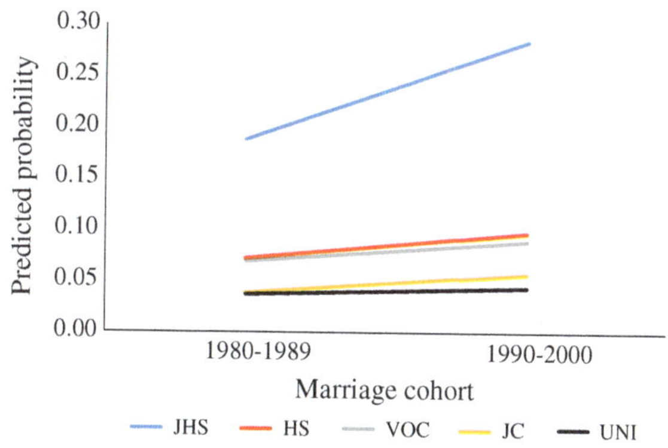

Fig. 3.6 Predicted probability of divorce within 10 years of marriage, by education and marriage cohort

women in more recent birth cohorts will, on average, have experienced shorter durations of exposure to the risk of divorce than their counterparts in earlier birth cohorts. We address this problem by using information on the timing of first marriage and divorce that is available in the 13th and 14th rounds of the NFS. Using these data, we describe educational differences in the probability of experiencing divorce within 10 years of marriage for two marriage cohorts—those marrying in the 1980s and those marrying in the 1990s. These analyses are limited to respondents whose first marriage occurred at least 10 years prior to the survey date. The results, presented in Fig. 3.6, indicate that the probability of divorce has increased somewhat for women in all educational groups and that women with a high school or vocational school education have higher divorce rates than junior college and university graduates. Again, the level of divorce and the pace of increase are most pronounced among women who did not complete high school. There is no statistical evidence, however, that differences across groups have grown over time. This pattern of findings is generally consistent with that presented by Raymo et al. (2013) who used these same data to examine trends in educational differences in divorce.

Chapter 4
Childbearing and Maternal Employment

4.1 Introduction

In this chapter, we describe trends in educational differences for several dimensions of childbearing including early childbearing, nonmarital childbearing, and bridal pregnancy. We also examine maternal employment. These analyses are based on the data described above in Sect. 3.2 and employ descriptive regression methods similar to those used in Chap. 3. This chapter concludes with a discussion of the results in both Chap. 3 and this chapter and suggestions for future research in this area.

4.2 Early Childbearing

Age at first birth is calculated from the fertility history modules in the NFS. Because detailed questions about childbearing refer only to women's current marriage (prior to the 14th NFS), these analyses do not include births in previous marriages for married women or any births for currently unmarried women. Figure 4.1 presents trends in the predicted probability of having a child by age 22. Early childbearing, defined in this way, has declined over time for all groups except college graduates. Because the probability of early motherhood for college graduates has remained constant at almost zero, the decline in early birth among high school graduates implies a narrowing of the gap between these two groups. However, women in the intermediate educational groups of vocational and junior college graduates have diverged from high school graduates. The difference between vocational school graduates and high school graduates is significantly larger in the 1970s birth cohort (relative to the 1940s cohort). For junior college graduates, the gap is larger from the 1950s cohort on and grew significantly in the 1960s birth cohort. In contrast to the U.S., where those with some college increasingly look like those with a high

J.M. Raymo and M. Iwasawa, *Diverging Destinies*,
Population Studies of Japan, DOI 10.1007/978-981-10-0185-7_4

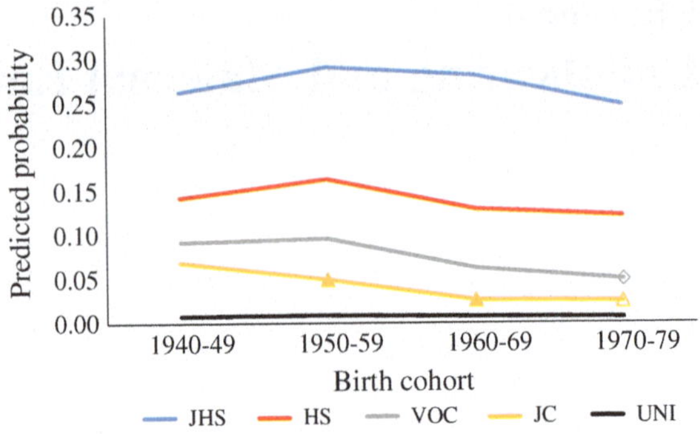

Fig. 4.1 Predicted probability of having a child by age 22, by education and birth cohort

school degree or less, Japanese women with two-year degrees increasingly resemble their more educated counterparts—at least with respect to the likelihood of early childbirth (and early marriage as shown above in Sect. 3.3). The odds ratios for early childbearing among women with two-year degrees (relative to high school graduates) fell from 0.60 (vocational school) and 0.45 (junior college) in the 1940s birth cohort to 0.37 and 0.20, respectively, in the 1970s birth cohort. The odds ratio for university graduates relative to high school graduates remained at 0.05 across cohorts.

As in our analysis of early marriage, the 22-year-old threshold for defining an early birth is arbitrary and it is important to keep in mind that the meaning of this threshold is not constant over time. Because the average age of first birth has increased substantially, rising from 26.1 in 1980 to 29.3 in 2010 (NIPSSR 2016), motherhood by age 22 is much more uncommon for more recent cohorts. The cumulative fertility rate at age 22 declined from 0.20 for the 1940 birth cohort to 0.08 for the 1985 birth cohort (NIPSSR 2016). Unlike the U.S., where teen childbearing is of considerable policy and scientific interest, very few Japanese women become parents as teenagers. We therefore present trends in the predicted age of first birth (among women who have had a child) in Fig. 4.2. Here, we see that age of motherhood has increased for all groups except women who did not

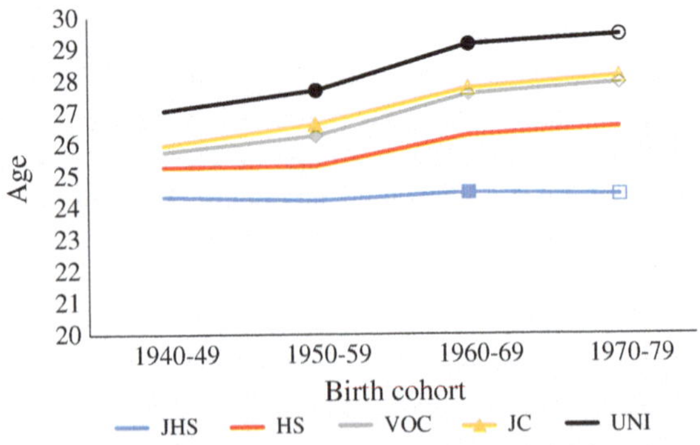

Fig. 4.2 Predicted age at first birth, by education and birth cohort

complete high school. It is also clear that the delay in childbearing has been more pronounced for women with more than a high school education. The difference between high school graduates and the three groups with more education is significantly larger in the 1950s, 1960s, and 1970s cohorts relative to the 1940s cohort. This gap also grew significantly in the 1960s for women with a junior college or university education, again suggesting that family bifurcation was particularly pronounced in the 1960s birth cohort. To the extent that age of motherhood per se, rather than the experience of early childbearing, is related to children's resources (McLanahan and Jacobsen 2015), these results are also consistent with a pattern of diverging destinies.

4.3 Nonmarital Childbearing

As noted in Chap. 2, the low level of extra-marital childbearing is one dimension of family behavior that sets Japan apart from most other low-fertility societies. To examine trends in this outcome, we constructed an indicator of nonmarital birth from the fertility and marriage history data, defining nonmarital births as those that occurred at least one month prior the reported month of marriage. Given the limitations of the fertility history data in the NFS, analyses of nonmarital childbearing do not include currently unmarried women and do not include births prior to married women's current marriage. The result of these data limitations will surely be an understatement of the prevalence of extra-marital births, but evidence that the rise in divorce has been similar across educational groups (Fig. 3.6) suggests that implications for our ability to evaluate trends in educational differences may be limited.

Figure 4.3 presents trends in predicted probabilities of experiencing a nonmarital birth. Three notable patterns are visible in this figure. The first is that the probability of nonmarital childbearing has grown rapidly among women who did not complete high school, providing further evidence of the increasingly distinctive behavior of this small group of women. Second, the level of nonmarital childbearing has

Fig. 4.3 Predicted probability of a nonmarital birth, by education and birth cohort

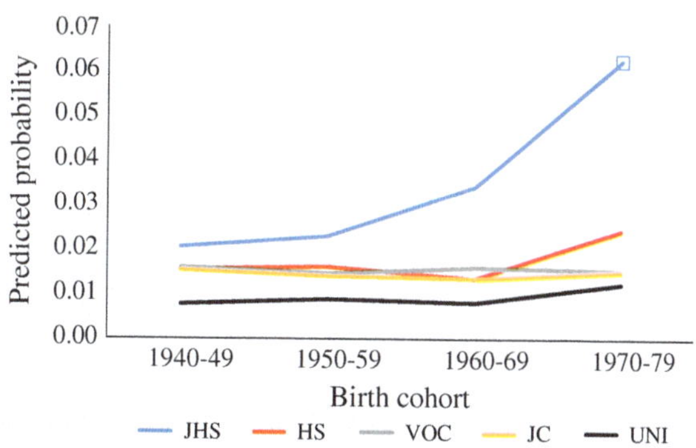

remained relatively stable at very low levels for all other groups of women and there is no statistical evidence of change in educational differences. The predicted probabilities of extra-marital childbearing are between 1 and 2 % across cohorts. The third pattern of note is the slight uptick in nonmarital childbearing among the most recent birth cohort. It may be that the seemingly sharp rise among high school graduates in the 1970s birth cohort represents the beginning of a divergence in the link between marriage and childbearing, but there is no statistical evidence for this and more time is needed to ascertain trends. This suggestive indication of change will be important to monitor going forward.

4.4 Bridal Pregnancy

Because the prevalence of nonmarital childbearing remains so low in Japan, bridal pregnancy is perhaps a more informative indicator of changing relationships between pregnancy and marriage. We again use information on the timing of marriage and first birth to define bridal pregnancy as cases in which the first birth occurs within the first seven months of marriage. This is the conventional approach used to define "shotgun marriages" (England et al. 2012).

Figure 4.4 presents trends, by educational attainment, in the predicted probability of bridal pregnancy. This pattern of change depicted in this figure is quite similar to the pattern of bifurcation in family outcomes described by McLanahan (2004) in her analyses of U.S. data. In the 1940s birth cohort, bridal pregnancy was relatively uncommon in all educational groups. University graduates were less likely than high school graduates to be pregnant at marriage, but the magnitude of the difference was small (3 vs. 6 %, respectively). The prevalence of bridal pregnancy has increased markedly across the educational distribution, but this change is most pronounced among women with a vocational school education or less. The gap between university graduates and high school graduates in the 1970s birth cohort was 15 % points, five times larger (in absolute terms) than the gap for the 1940s birth cohort. However, change in the relative difference is small and not

Fig. 4.4 Predicted probability of bridal pregnancy, by education and birth cohort

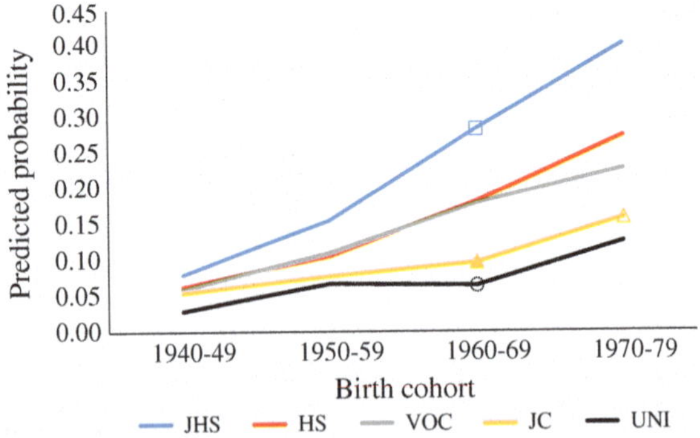

statistically different from zero, except for a significant growth in the gap for the 1960s birth cohort (relative to the gap for the 1950s birth cohort). This is one of the only examples in our analyses of a significant change across successive cohorts that does not correspond to a significant difference with the earliest cohort. Again, it appears that the 1960s birth cohort experienced particularly pronounced socioeconomic bifurcation in family behavior.

It is also interesting to note the pattern of bifurcation among women with intermediate levels of education. Those who completed vocational school closely resemble high school graduates (at least until the 1970s birth cohort), while junior college graduates more closely resemble university graduates. We are not aware of any research that carefully considers the composition of these two groups (with respect to background compositional characteristics and aspirations with respect to work and family), but further consideration of differences and similarities in family (and work) behavior relative to those with higher and lower education could shed light on this. We revisit this point below in the discussion section.

4.5 Maternal Employment

The NFS questionnaires have consistently ascertained mothers' employment status when their first child was one year old. Figure 4.5 presents trends, by educational attainment, in the predicted probability of this important indicator of stable maternal employment. As with bridal pregnancy, trends are generally consistent with a pattern of diverging destinies. The probability of employment has increased across cohorts for all women, but the increase that has been most pronounced among women is university education (and among vocational school graduates). Among recent mothers in the 1940s birth cohort, there were essentially no educational differences in employment, with only 5–6 % of women at any education level employed at the time of their first child's first birthday. Japanese mothers remain unlikely to be employed (relative to their counterparts in the U.S. and other developed countries), but university-educated mothers in the 1970s birth cohort

Fig. 4.5 Predicted probability of employment one year after first birth, by education and birth cohort

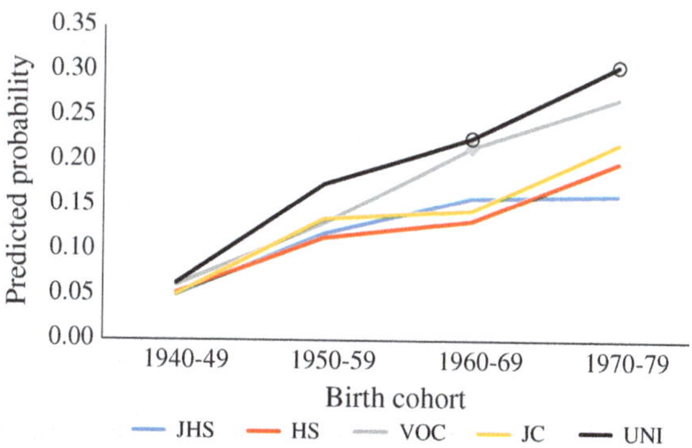

were 11 % points more likely to be employed than their counterparts with a high school education. This represents a statistically significant divergence from the first cohort.

In light of earlier discussion of the two intermediate educational groups, it is interesting to note that, with respect to employment, vocational school graduates more closely resemble university graduates, while junior college graduates continue to resemble mothers with a high school education. It may be that these intermediately educated women are increasingly comprised of two groups—those with stronger family orientation and those with stronger work orientation, with the former more likely to attend junior college and the latter more likely to attend vocational school.

Considering the tendency for mothers to work low-paying, part-time jobs (Raymo and Lim 2011; Yu 2002), employment per se may not be the best measure of mothers' work status when evaluating evidence of diverging destinies. We therefore replicate the analyses in Fig. 4.5 using regular, full-time employment (*seishain*) as the outcome of interest. Again, this measure refers to mothers' employment at the time of her first child's first birthday. Figure 4.6 shows that the pattern of change is similar, but more pronounced, than that for employment. The predicted probability of being in regular employment has increased for all educational groups, but the change has been much more rapid among university graduates.

Differences were minor in the 1940s cohort, ranging from 3 % for mothers who did not complete high school to 6 % for those who graduated from university. In the 1970s cohort, the predicted probability of full-time, regular employment reached 24 % for university graduates, 13 % points higher than for high school graduates. Again, as in many of these analyses, the relative difference has changed little but growth in the absolute difference between the two groups is striking. It is interesting to note that, the similarity between university and vocational school graduates seen in Fig. 4.5 is less pronounced when we focus on full-time regular employment. When it comes to career-type employment, the most highly educated mothers are increasingly behaving differently than their less-educated counterparts. This pattern of change is similar to that documented in the U.S. and may have important

Fig. 4.6 Predicted probability of regular employment one year after first birth, by education and birth cohort

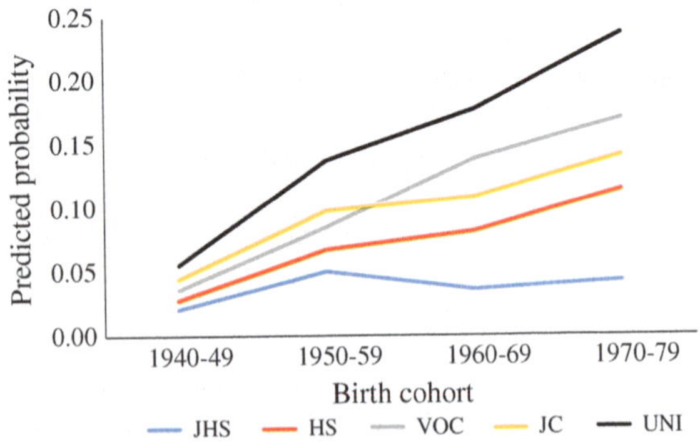

implications for trends in disparities in children's economic resources. Going forward, it will be interesting and important to focus on the extent to which this shift in the relative likelihood of continued employment contributes to growing differences in children's well-being in Japan where social norms have long emphasized the importance of mothers' nurturing and hands-on investment in children's educational success.

4.6 Discussion

In this manuscript, we have sought to provide a broad descriptive evaluation of evidence for a pattern of diverging destinies in Japan using a single data source. In doing so, we have synthesized and extended a number of related studies that we have published over the past decade. Evaluating evidence of growing educational differences in family behavior in Japan is important for both theoretical and substantive reasons. Theoretically, evaluating the relevance of diverging destinies in the Japanese context provides an important assessment of the generality of a provocative and influential framework that has been developed primarily with reference to family trends in the U.S. and other low-fertility Western populations.

Japan is important because there are several reasons to both expect and not expect similar patterns of change. As described in Chap. 2, reasons to expect a pattern of diverging destinies in Japan include limited public support for families, growing economic inequality, bifurcation of the labor market into regular and nonstandard employment, and increasing educational attainment for women. Reasons to expect that family bifurcation is unlikely in Japan include a history of a very homogeneous family life course, a very distinctive contraceptive environment, and a highly asymmetric gender division of labor within the family. Our focus on Japan thus has the potential to shed light on the conditions under which specific aspects of family change central to the diverging destinies literature do or do not occur.

At a more substantive level, our focus on diverging destinies is a useful contribution to research on stratification and inequality in Japan. There is a great deal of academic and policy interest in evidence of growing stratification and inequality, but systematic, theoretically grounded efforts to link variation in children's resources to family behavior are limited. Indeed, it appears that McLanahan's research on family bifurcation and its implications for inequality in the U.S. and other low-fertility societies has yet to have any meaningful influence on family scholarship published in Japan. We therefore view this study as an initial effort to address this gap in the literature on Japanese family change and hope that, by examining trends in educational differences in family behavior, we are able to provide some useful insights into the likely contributions (or lack thereof) of family behavior to variation in resources and well-being at both the individual and societal level.

The results of our analyses are mixed. Taken as a whole, our descriptive analyses clearly demonstrate that evidence for the marked educational bifurcation in family behavior that has been observed in the U.S. is limited in Japan. This is perhaps not surprising in light of evidence that the pattern of diverging destinies appears to be particularly pronounced in the U.S. (McLanahan and Jacobsen 2015). At the same time, it is clear that educational differences in some family behaviors, especially those related to childbearing and employment, have indeed grown over time. Particularly striking is clear growth in educational gradients in bridal pregnancy and maternal employment. In both cases, the pattern of change is consistent with expectations based on the notion of diverging destinies—bridal pregnancy is increasingly concentrated among women with lower levels of education whereas (standard) employment following childbirth is increasingly concentrated among more highly educated women.

We consider this descriptive summary of trends in family behavior to be a useful contribution to our understanding of linkages between family behavior and inequality, but recognize that our study is limited in many important ways. Many of these limitations reflect the nature of the available data. As described above, the lack of information on the timing of marital dissolution and the duration of non-marital cohabiting unions makes rigorous analyses of these outcomes difficult. Similarly, the absence of information on childbearing outcomes for formerly married women precluded analysis of a growing segment of women that we know to be concentrated at lower levels of education. This is the price that one must pay for the long temporal coverage provided the NFS data. We are not aware of any other data source that would allow for a more comprehensive analysis of trends over time in educational differences in family behavior. Census data provide no information on the timing of family transitions and Vital Statistics data do not contain information on educational attainment.

Other important limitations of the data that we have examined include the difficulty of comparing static educational categories over time and the absence of any direct measures of children's resources or well-being. As noted above, rapid changes in women's educational attainment imply that a given level of education means something different for earlier cohorts than it does for later cohorts. We have emphasized the increasingly select nature of women with less than a high school education and have argued that patterns of family change for these women should be evaluated with caution in light of their increasingly selectivity. Similar concerns about changing patters of self-selection hold for women at higher levels of education. For example, it is particularly important to consider the ways in which the process by which young women select themselves into junior college versus university have changed over time. Unlike McLanahan (2004), who was able to circumvent this problem by using data on years of education that allowed for construction of relative levels of educational attainment, we were limited to fixed educational categories when using the NFS data.

We also restricted our focus to the behavior of adult women because the NFS surveys do not contain information about the circumstances of children. This is a particularly important limitation given the explicit focus on children's resources in the diverging destinies literature. We recognize this as a major limitation of our study and a potentially important area of research going forward and stress that the value of this manuscript lies in the presentation of evidence on Japanese women's family behavior that can be compared with the growing body of research on related outcomes in the U.S. and elsewhere.

Although the diverging destinies literature tends to focus on differences between the highly educated and their counterparts at the lower end of the educational distribution, those with intermediate levels of education are also of interest. Documenting patterns of family change for this group can provide insights not only into the likely patterns of divergence in children's resources, but also into the factors that underlie observed patterns of change. For example, in the U.S., the growing similarity of those in the middle and the lower end of the educational distribution has been linked to changing labor market circumstances that are thought to affect the two groups in similar ways (Cherlin 2011). On this point, our analyses of Japanese data again provide a mixed picture. For outcomes related to the timing of family formation (early marriage and early childbearing), both vocational school and junior college graduates increasingly resemble university-educated women rather than women with lower levels of education. However, with respect to the nature of family formation (e.g., nonmarital cohabitation, bridal pregnancy) and marital dissolution, vocational school graduates increasingly resemble high school graduates while junior college graduates look more like women with a university degree. This pattern is reversed for maternal employment, with vocational school graduates more similar to university graduates and women who attended junior college more similar to high school graduates. These patterns suggest changing patterns of selection that result in concentration of women with stronger work orientation (perhaps along with more precarious economic circumstances) among those attending vocational school and a stronger family orientation among those attending junior college. In light of the rapid changes in the educational composition of the female population in Japan, we consider further efforts to evaluate these speculative hypotheses and their implications for individual and family well-being a fruitful avenue for subsequent research on the link between education, economic change, family change, and inequality in Japan.

References

Aassve, A., Betti, G., Mazzuco, S., & Mencarini, L. (2007). Marital disruption and economic well-being: A comparative analysis. *Journal of the Royal Statistical Society: Series A (Statistics in Society), 170*(3), 781–799.

Abe, A. (2008). *Children's poverty: A study of inequality in Japan*. Tokyo: Iwanami Shoten. (in Japanese).

Abe, A., & Oishi, A. (2005). Social security and the economic circumstances of single-mother households. In National Institute of Population and Social Security Research (Ed.), *Social security and households with children* (pp. 143–161). Tokyo: Tokyo Daigaku Shuppankai (in Japanese).

Akabayashi, H. (2006). The labor supply of married women and spousal tax deductions in Japan—a structural estimation. *Review of Economics of the Household, 4*(4), 349–378.

Akaishi, C. (2011). Single mothers. In K. Fujimura-Fanselow (Ed.), *Transforming Japan: How feminism and diversity are making a difference* (pp. 121–30). New York: The Feminist Press at the City University of New York.

Akerlof, G. A., Yellen, J. L., & Katz, M. L. (1996). An analysis of out-of-wedlock childbearing in the United States. *The Quarterly Journal of Economics, 111*(2), 277–317.

Amato, P. R. (2000). The consequences of divorce for adults and children. *Journal of Marriage and Family, 62*(4), 1269–1287.

Amato, P. R. (2005). The impact of family formation change on the cognitive, social, and emotional well-being of the next generation. *The Future of Children, 15*(2), 75–96.

Amato, P. R., & James, S. (2010). Divorce in Europe and the United States: Commonalities and differences across nations. *Family Science, 1*(1), 2–13.

Amato, P. R., & Sobolewski, J. M. (2001). The effects of divorce and marital discord on adult children's psychological well-being. *American Sociological Review, 66*(6), 900–921.

Astone, N. M., & McLanahan, S. S. (1991). Family structure, parental practices and high school completion. *American Sociological Review, 56*(3), 309–320.

Atoh, M. (2001). Very low fertility in Japan and value change hypotheses. *Review of Population and Social Policy, 10*, 1–21.

Atoh, M., Kandiah, V., & Ivanov, S. (2004). The second demographic transition in Asia? Comparative analysis of the low fertility situation in East and South-East Asian countries. *The Japanese Journal of Population, 2*(1), 42–75.

Avellar, S., & Smock, P. J. (2005). The economic consequences of the dissolution of cohabiting unions. *Journal of Marriage and Family, 67*(2), 315–327.

Becker, G. S. (1981). *A treatise on the family*. Cambridge, MA: Harvard University Press.

Beller, E. (2009). Bringing intergenerational social mobility research into the twenty-first century: Why mothers matter. *American Sociological Review, 74*(4), 507–528.

Biblarz, T. J., & Gottainer, G. (2000). Family structure and children's success: A comparison of widowed and divorced single-mother families. *Journal of Marriage and Family, 62*(2), 533–548.

J.M. Raymo and M. Iwasawa, *Diverging Destinies*,
Population Studies of Japan, DOI 10.1007/978-981-10-0185-7

Biblarz, T. J., & Raftery, A. E. (1993). The effects of family disruption on social mobility. *American Sociological Review, 58*(1), 97–109.

Biblarz, T. J., Raftery, A. E., & Bucur, A. (1997). Family structure and social mobility. *Social Forces, 75*(4), 1319–1341.

Boling, P. (2007). Policies to support working mothers and children in Japan. In F. M. Rosenbluth (Ed.), *The political economy of Japan's low fertility* (pp. 131–154). Stanford, CA: Stanford University Press.

Brady, D., & Burroway, R. (2012). Targeting, universalism, and single-mother poverty: A multilevel analysis across 18 affluent democracies. *Demography, 49*(2), 719–746.

Brinton, M. C. (1992). Christmas cakes and wedding cakes: The social organization of Japanese women's life course. In T. S. Lebra (Ed.), *Japanese social organization* (pp. 79–107). Honolulu, HI: University of Hawaii Press.

Brinton, M. C. (1993). *Women and the economic miracle: Gender and work in postwar Japan*. Berkeley, CA: University of California Press.

Brinton, M. C. (2011). *Lost in transition*. New York: Cambridge University Press.

Bumpass, L., Choe, M. K., Tsuya, N. O., & Rindfuss, R. R. (2010). *Role overload: Preference for wives' employment hours in Japan*. Paper presented at the Annual Meeting of the Population Association of America. Dallas, TX (April 15–17).

Burstein, N. R. (2007). Economic influences on marriage and divorce. *Journal of Policy Analysis and Management, 26*(2), 387–429.

Carlson, M. J., & Corcoran, M. E. (2001). Family structure and children's behavioral and cognitive outcomes. *Journal of Marriage and Family, 63*(3), 779–792.

Carlson, M. J., & Furstenberg, F. F. (2006). The prevalence and correlates of multipartnered fertility among urban US parents. *Journal of Marriage and Family, 68*(3), 718–732.

Carlson, M., Raymo, J. M., VanOrman, A., & Lim, S-J. (2014). *Cross-national differences in early family instability by socioeconomic status*. Paper presented at the International Sociological Association World Congress (RC28), Yokohama, Japan (July).

Cavanagh, S. E., & Huston, A. C. (2006). Family instability and children's early problem behavior. *Social Forces, 85*(1), 551–581.

Chan, T. W., & Halpin, B. (2005). The instability of divorce risk factors in the UK. In *British Society for Population Studies Annual Conference,* Canterbury, UK.

Cherlin, A. J. (2009). *The marriage-go-round: The state of marriage and the family in America today*. New York: Alfred A. Knopf.

Cherlin, A. J. (2010). Demographic trends in the United States: A review of research in the 2000s. *Journal of Marriage and Family, 72*(3), 403–419.

Cherlin, A. J. (2011). Between poor and prosperous: Do the family patterns of moderately educated Americans deserve a closer look? In M. J. Carlson & P. England (Eds.), *Social class and changing families in an unequal America* (pp. 68–84). Stanford CA: Stanford University Press.

Cherlin, A. J., Chase-Lansdale, P. L., & McRae, C. (1998). Effects of parental divorce on mental health throughout the life course. *American Sociological Review, 63*(2), 239–249.

Conger, R. D., Conger, K. J., Elder, G. H., Lorenz, F. O., Simons, R. L., & Whitbeck, L. B. (1992). A family process model of economic hardship and adjustment of early adolescent boys. *Child Development, 63*(3), 526–541.

Cooper, C. E., McLanahan, S. S., Meadows, S. O., & Brooks-Gunn, J. (2009). Family structure transitions and maternal parenting stress. *Journal of Marriage and Family, 71*(3), 558–574.

De Graaf, P. M., & Kalmijn, M. (2006). Change and stability in the social determinants of divorce: A comparison of marriage cohorts in the Netherlands. *European Sociological Review, 22*(5), 561–572.

Duncan, G. J., Yeung, W. J., Brooks-Gunn, J., & Smith, J. R. (1998). How much does childhood poverty affect the life chances of children? *American Sociological Review, 63*(3), 406–423.

Edin, K., Kefalas, M. J., & Reed, J. M. (2004). A peek inside the black box: What marriage means for poor unmarried parents. *Journal of Marriage and Family, 66*(4), 1007–1014.

Ellwood, D. T., & Jencks, C. (2004). The uneven spread of single-parent families: What do we know? Where do we look for answers? In K. Neckerman (Ed.), *Social inequality* (pp. 3–78). New York: Russell Sage Foundation.

England, P., Shafer, E. F., & Wu, L. L. (2012). Premarital conceptions, postconception ("shotgun") marriages, and premarital first births: Education gradients in US cohorts of white and black women born 1925–1959. *Demographic Research, 27*, 153–166.

Esping-Andersen, G. (2007). Sociological explanations of changing income distributions. *American Behavioral Scientist, 50*(5), 639–658.

Fomby, P., & Cherlin, A. J. (2007). Family instability and child well-being. *American Sociological Review, 72*(2), 181–204.

Fukuda, S. (2013). The changing role of women's earnings in marriage formation in Japan. *The Annals of the American Academy of Political and Social Science, 646*(1), 107–128.

Fukuda, S., & Raymo, J. M. (2015). *New patterns of educational differentials and assortative mating after 2005 in Japan: A shift in the foundations of marriage?* Paper presented Conference on Education and Reproduction in Low-Fertility Settings. Vienna Institute of Demography. (December).

Futagami, S. (2010). *Non-standard employment in Japan: Gender dimensions*. Discussion Paper DP/200/2010. Geneva: International Institute for Labour Studies.

Genda, Y., Kondo, A., & Ohta, S. (2010). Long-term effects of a recession at labor market entry in Japan and the United States. *Journal of Human Resources, 45*(1), 157–196.

Goldstein, J. R., & Kenney, C. T. (2001). Marriage delayed or marriage forgone? New cohort forecasts of first marriage for US women. *American Sociological Review, 66*(4), 506–519.

Gottschalk, P., & Danziger, S. (2005). Inequality of wage rates, earnings and family income in the United States, 1975–2002. *Review of Income and Wealth, 51*(2), 231–254.

Gould, E. D., & Paserman, M. D. (2003). Waiting for Mr. Right: Rising inequality and declining marriage rates. *Journal of Urban Economics, 53*(2), 257–281.

Greenwood, J., Guner, N., Kocharkov, G., & Santos, C. (2014). *Marry your like: Assortative mating and income inequality*. NBER Working Paper 19829, Cambridge, MA: National Bureau of Economic Research.

Harknett, K., & Knab, J. (2007). More kin, less support: Multipartnered fertility and perceived support among mothers. *Journal of Marriage and Family, 69*(1), 237–253.

Härkönen, J., & Dronkers, J. (2006). Stability and change in the educational gradient of divorce: A comparison of seventeen countries. *European Sociological Review, 22*(5), 501–517.

Heuveline, P., & Timberlake, J. M. (2004). The role of cohabitation in family formation: The United States in comparative perspective. *Journal of Marriage and Family, 66*(5), 1214–1230.

Heuveline, P., & Weinshenker, M. (2008). The international child poverty gap: Does demography matter? *Demography, 45*(1), 173–191.

Hodge, R. W., & Ogawa, N. (1992). *Fertility change in contemporary Japan*. Chicago: University of Chicago Press.

Hoem, J. M. (1997). Educational gradients in divorce risks in Sweden in recent decades. *Population Studies, 51*(1), 19–27.

Houseman, S., & Osawa, M. (2003). The growth of nonstandard employment in Japan and the United States. In S. Houseman & M. Osawa (Eds.), *Nonstandard work in developed economies: Causes and consequences* (pp. 175–214). Kalamazoo, MI: WE Upjohn Institute for Employment Research.

Ishida, H., & Motegi, A. (2014). *Educational assortative mating among unmarried and married couples in Japan and the United States*. Panel Survey Project Discussion Paper Series No. 72. Tokyo: Institute of Social Sciences, University of Tokyo.

Iwasawa, M. (2013). An analysis of marriage decline and changes in marriage structures in Japan since the 1970s using multiple decrement life tables on first marriage. *Journal of Population Problems, 69*(2), 1–34. (in Japanese).

Iwasawa, M., & Kamata, K. (2014). Marriage preceded by pregnancy and women's employment. *Japan Labor Review, 11*(4), 21–51.

Jackson, A. P., Brooks-Gunn, J., Huang, C., & Glassman, M. (2000). Single mothers in low-wage jobs: Financial strain, parenting, and preschoolers' outcomes. *Child Development, 71*(5), 1409–1423.

Johnson, D. R., & Wu, J. (2002). An empirical test of crisis, social selection, and role explanations of the relationship between marital disruption and psychological distress: A pooled time-series analysis of four-wave panel data. *Journal of Marriage and Family, 64*(1), 211–224.

Kalil, A., & Ryan, R. M. (2010). Mothers' economic conditions and sources of support in fragile families. *The Future of Children, 20*(2), 39–61.

Kalmijn, M. (2013). The educational gradient in marriage: A comparison of 25 European countries. *Demography, 50*(4), 1499–1520.

Kamp Dush, C. M., Cohan, C. L., & Amato, P. R. (2003). The relationship between cohabitation and marital quality and stability: Change across cohorts? *Journal of Marriage and Family, 65* (3), 539–549.

Katō, A. (2005). Determinants of divorce: Family structure, social class, and economic growth. In Japan Society for Family Sociology (Ed.), *Cohort comparison analysis of family change in postwar Japan* (pp. 77–90). Tokyo: Japan Society for Family Sociology. (in Japanese).

Kennedy, S., & Bumpass, L. (2008). Cohabitation and children's living arrangements: New estimates from the United States. *Demographic Research, 19*, 1663–1692.

Kennedy, S., & Thomson, E. (2010). Children's experiences of family disruption in Sweden: Differentials by parent education over three decades. *Demographic Research, 23*, 479–508.

Kiernan, K. (2001). The rise of cohabitation and childbearing outside marriage in Western Europe. *International Journal of Law, Policy and the Family, 15*(1), 1–21.

Kohara, M. (2007). Is the full-time housewife a symbol of a wealthy family? *Japanese Economy, 34*(4), 25–56.

Kondo, A. (2014). *Recession and low fertility: Analysis of unemployment rates, fertility rates, and marriage rates using prefectural panel data.* Unpublished manuscript. (in Japanese).

Kost, K., Singh, S., Vaughan, B., Trussell, J., & Bankole, A. (2008). Estimates of contraceptive failure from the 2002 National Survey of Family Growth. *Contraception, 77*(1), 10–21.

Lesthaeghe, R. (1995). The second demographic transition in Western countries: An interpretation. In K. O. Mason & A.-M. Jensen (Eds.), *Gender and family change in industrialized countries* (pp. 17–62). Oxford, UK: Clarendon Press.

Lesthaeghe, R. (2010). The unfolding story of the second demographic transition. *Population and Development Review, 36*(2), 211–251.

Lesthaeghe, R., & Moors, G. (2000). Recent trends in fertility and household formation in the industrialized world. *Review of Population and Social Policy, 9*(1), 121–170.

Lim, S.-J., & Raymo, J. M. (2014). Nonstandard work and educational differentials in married women's employment in Japan: Patterns of continuity and change. *International Journal of Sociology, 44*(3), 84–107.

Lundberg, S., & Pollak, R. A. (2013). *Cohabitation and the uneven retreat from marriage in the US, 1950–2010.* NBER Working Paper 19413. Cambridge, MA: National Bureau of Economic Research.

Manning, W. D., Brown, S. L., & Stykes, J. B. (2014). Family complexity among children in the United States. *The Annals of the American Academy of Political and Social Science, 654*(1), 48–65.

Martin, M. A. (2006). Family structure and income inequality in families with children, 1976 to 2000. *Demography, 43*(3), 421–445.

Martin, S. P. (2006). Trends in marital dissolution by women's education in the United States. *Demographic Research, 15*, 537–560.

Martin, S. P., & Parashar, S. (2006). Women's changing attitudes toward divorce, 1974–2002: Evidence for an educational crossover. *Journal of Marriage and Family, 68*(1), 29–40.

Matsueda, R. L., & Heimer, K. (1987). Race, family structure, and delinquency: A test of differential association and social control theories. *American Sociological Review, 52*(6), 826–840.

Matsuo, H. (2001). *Is Japan a second demographic transition country? Observations based on union, first birth status and values in The Netherlands and Japan.* Paper presented at Conference on the Second Demographic Transition in Europe. Bad Herrenalb, Germany (June).

Matysiak, A., Styrc, M., & Vignoli, D. (2014). The educational gradient in marital disruption: A meta-analysis of European research findings. *Population Studies, 68*(2), 197–215.

McDonald, P. (2000a). Gender equity in theories of fertility transition. *Population and Development Review, 26*(3), 427–439.

McDonald, P. (2000b). Gender equity, social institutions and the future of fertility. *Journal of Population Research, 17*(1), 1–16.

McDonald, P. (2009). Explanations of low fertility in East Asia: A comparative perspective. In G. Jones, P. T. Straughan, & A. Chan (Eds.), *Ultra-low fertility in Pacific Asia: Trends, causes, and policy issues* (pp. 23–39). Oxford, UK: Routledge.

McLanahan, S. (2004). Diverging destinies: How children are faring under the second demographic transition. *Demography, 41*(4), 607–627.

McLanahan, S. (2009). Fragile families and the reproduction of poverty. *The Annals of the American Academy of Political and Social Science, 621*(1), 111–131.

McLanahan, S., & Jacobsen, W. (2015). Diverging destinies revisited. In P.R. Amato, A. Booth, S. M McHale, & J. Van Hook (Eds.), *Families in an era of increasing inequality* (pp. 3–23). New York: Springer.

McLanahan, S., & Percheski, C. (2008). Family structure and the reproduction of inequalities. *Annual Review of Sociology, 34*, 257–276.

McLanahan, S., & Sandefur, G. (1994). *Growing up with a single parent. What hurts, what helps.* Cambridge, MA: Harvard University Press.

Meadows, S. O., McLanahan, S. S., & Brooks-Gunn, J. (2007). Parental depression and anxiety and early childhood behavior problems across family types. *Journal of Marriage and Family, 69*(5), 1162–1177.

Meadows, S. O., McLanahan, S. S., & Brooks-Gunn, J. (2008). Stability and change in family structure and maternal health trajectories. *American Sociological Review, 73*(2), 314–334.

Milkie, M. A., Mattingly, M. J., Nomaguchi, K. M., Bianchi, S. M., & Robinson, J. P. (2004). The time squeeze: Parental statuses and feelings about time with children. *Journal of Marriage and Family, 66*(3), 739–761.

Moriguchi, C., & Saez, E. (2008). The evolution of income concentration in Japan, 1886–2005: Evidence from income tax statistics. *The Review of Economics and Statistics, 90*(4), 713–734.

Morris, M., & Western, B. (1999). Inequality in earnings at the close of the twentieth century. *Annual Review of Sociology, 25*, 623–657.

Musick, K., England, P., Edgington, S., & Kangas, N. (2009). Education differences in intended and unintended fertility. *Social Forces, 88*(2), 543–572.

Musick, K., & Michelmore, K. (2015). Change in the stability of marital and cohabiting unions following the birth of a child. *Demography, 52*(5), 1463–1485.

Nagase, N. (2002). Marriage timing and the effect of increase in non-standard employment among the youth in Japan. *Journal of Population Problems, 58*(2), 22–35.

Nagase, N. (2014). The effect of a mandatory short hours policy on first birth, employment, and fertility intentions: An analysis based on a policy induced natural experiment. *Demographic Research, 37*(1), 27–53. (in Japanese).

Nagase, N., & Moriizumi, R. (2013). Why hasn't employment continuation after first birth increased? An cohort comparison based on the 12th National Fertility Survey. *Social Science Research on Everyday Life, 20*, 19–36.

National Institute of Population and Social Security Research. (2012). *The fourteenth Japanese National Fertility Survey in 2010, marriage process and fertility of Japanese married couples, highlights of the survey results on married couples.* Retrieved on March 1, 2015 (http://www.ipss.go.jp/site-ad/index_english/nfs14/Nfs14_Couples_Eng.pdf). (in Japanese).

National Institute of Population and Social Security Research. (2015). *Latest demographic statistics*. Tokyo: National Institute of Population and Social Security Research. (in Japanese).

OECD. (2016a). Income distribution and poverty database. https://stats.oecd.org/Index.aspx?DataSetCode=IDD

OECD. (2016b). Family database. http://www.oecd.org/els/family/database.htm

Ogura, S., & Kadoda, T. (2008). The role of the youth labor market and public policy in shaping fertility behavior: An analysis of municipality panel data. *Economic Analysis, 59*, 330–339. (in Japanese).

Ohtake, F. (2005). *Inequality in Japan: The illusion and the future of a stratified society*. Tokyo: Nihon Keizai Shinbunsha. (in Japanese).

Ohtake, F., Kohara, M., Okuyama, N., & Yamada, K. (2013). Growing inequalities and their impacts in Japan. Gini Country Reports. http://gini-research.org/system/uploads/449/original/Japan.pdf?1370090592

Ono, H. (2003). Women's economic standing, marriage timing, and cross-national contexts of gender. *Journal of Marriage and Family, 65*(2), 275–286.

Ono, H. (2009). Husbands' and wives' education and divorce in the United States and Japan, 1946–2000. *Journal of Family History, 34*(3), 292–322.

Oppenheimer, V. K. (1988). A theory of marriage timing. *American Journal of Sociology, 94*(3), 563–591.

Oppenheimer, V. K. (1997). Women's employment and the gain to marriage: The specialization and trading model. *Annual Review of Sociology, 23*, 431–453.

Oppenheimer, V. K., Kalmijn, M., & Lim, N. (1997). Men's career development and marriage timing during a period of rising inequality. *Demography, 34*(3), 311–330.

Osawa, M., Kim, M. J., & Kingston, J. (2013). Precarious work in Japan. *American Behavioral Scientist, 57*(3), 309–334.

Osborne, C., & Ankrum, N. (2015). Understanding today's changing families. *Family Court Review, 53*(2), 221–232.

Osborne, C., Manning, W. D., & Smock, P. J. (2007). Married and cohabiting parents' relationship stability: A focus on race and ethnicity. *Journal of Marriage and Family, 69*(5), 1345–1366.

Osborne, C., & McLanahan, S. (2007). Partnership instability and child well-being. *Journal of Marriage and Family, 69*(4), 1065–1083.

Park, H., & Raymo, J. M. (2013). Divorce in Korea: Trends and educational differentials. *Journal of Marriage and Family, 75*(1), 110–126.

Perelli-Harris, B., & Amos-Lyons, M. (2014). *Partnership patterns in the United States and across Europe: "Diverging destinies" or "diverging contexts"?* ESRC Working Paper 53. Center for Population Change, Southampton University.

Perelli-Harris, B., & Gerber, T. P. (2011). Nonmarital childbearing in Russia: Second demographic transition or pattern of disadvantage? *Demography, 48*(1), 317–342.

Perelli-Harris, B., Sigle-Rushton, W., Kreyenfeld, M., Lappegård, T., Keizer, R., & Berghammer, C. (2010). The educational gradient of childbearing within cohabitation in Europe. *Population and Development Review, 36*(4), 775–801.

Piotrowski, M., Kalleberg, A., & Rindfuss, R. R. (2015). Contingent work rising: Implications for the timing of marriage in Japan. *Journal of Marriage and Family, 77*(5), 1039–1056.

Powell, M. A., & Parcel, T. L. (1997). Effects of family structure on the earnings attainment process: Differences by gender. *Journal of Marriage and the Family, 59*(2), 419–433.

Raley, R. K., & Bumpass, L. (2003). The topography of the divorce plateau: Levels and trends in union stability in the United States after 1980. *Demographic Research, 8*, 245–260.

Raymo, J. M. (2003). Educational attainment and the transition to first marriage among Japanese women. *Demography, 40*(1), 83–103.

Raymo, J. M. (2008). Educational differentials in divorce in Japan: Evidence from multiple data sources. In National Institute of Population and Social Security Research (Eds.), *Demographic research on divorce and remarriage in the context of low fertility*. Tokyo: National Institute of Population and Social Security Research.

Raymo, J. M. (2015a). Second demographic transition. In J. D. Wright (Ed.), *The International encyclopedia of social and behavioral sciences* (2nd ed., pp. 346–348). Oxford, UK: Elsevier.
Raymo, J. M. (2015b). Single mothers' happiness, health, and economic well-being. in *Well-being in households with children* (pp. 100−119). Tokyo: Japan Institute for Labour Policy and Training. (in Japanese).
Raymo, J. M. (2016). Single motherhood and children's health and school performance in Japan. *Marriage and Family Review*, *5*(1–2), 64–88.
Raymo, J., Carlson, M., VanOrman, A., Lim, S., Perelli-Harris, B., & Iwasawa, M. (2015). Educational differences in early childbearing: A cross-national comparative study. *Demographic Research, 33*(3), 65–92.
Raymo, J. M., Fukuda, S., & Iwasawa, M. (2013). Educational differences in divorce in Japan. *Demographic Research, 28*, 177–206.
Raymo, J. M., & Iwasawa, M. (2005). Marriage market mismatches in Japan: An alternative view of the relationship between women's education and marriage. *American Sociological Review, 70*(5), 801–822.
Raymo, J. M., & Iwasawa, M. (2008). Bridal pregnancy and spouse pairing patterns in Japan. *Journal of Marriage and Family, 70*(4), 847–860.
Raymo, J. M., Iwasawa, M., & Bumpass, L. (2004). Marital dissolution in Japan: Recent trends and patterns. *Demographic Research, 11*, 395–420.
Raymo, J. M., Iwasawa, M., & Bumpass, L. (2009). Cohabitation and family formation in Japan. *Demography, 46*(4), 785–803.
Raymo, J. M., & Lim, S-J. (2011). A new look at married women's labor force transitions in Japan. *Social Science Research, 40*(2), 460–472.
Raymo, J. M., Musick, K., & Iwasawa, M. (2015). Gender equity, opportunity costs of parenthood, and educational differences in unintended first births: Insights from Japan. *Population Research and Policy Review, 34*(2), 179–199.
Raymo, J. M., Park, H., Iwasawa, M., & Zhou, Y. (2014). Single motherhood, living arrangements, and time with children in Japan. *Journal of Marriage and Family, 76*(4), 843–861.
Raymo, J. M., & Shibata, A. (2014). *Economic uncertainty and fertility: Insights from Japan*. Paper presented at the Annual Meeting of the American Sociological Association, San Francisco (August).
Raymo, J. M., & Xie, Y. (2000). Temporal and regional variation in the strength of educational homogamy. *American Sociological Review, 65*(5), 773–781.
Raymo, J. M., & Zhou, Y. (2012). Living arrangements and the well-being of single mothers in Japan. *Population Research and Policy Review, 31*(5), 727–749.
Rebick, M. (2005). *The Japanese employment system: Adapting to a new economic environment*. Oxford: Oxford University Press.
Rendall, M., Aracil, E., Bagavos, C., Couet, C., DeRose, A., DiGiulio, P., et al. (2010). Increasingly heterogeneous ages at first birth by education in southern European and anglo-american family-policy regimes: A seven-country comparison by birth cohort. *Population Studies, 64*(3), 209–227.
Rendall, M., Couer, C., Lappegard, T., Robert-Bobée, I., Ronsen, M., & Smallwood, S. (2005). First births by age and education in Britain, France and Norway. *Population Trends, 121*, 27–34.
Rendall, M. S., Ekert-Jaffé, O., Joshi, H., Lynch, K., & Mougin, R. (2009). Universal versus economically polarized change in age at first birth: A French-British comparison. *Population and Development Review, 35*(1), 89–115.
Rendall, M. S., & Smallwood, S. (2003). Higher qualifications, first-birth timing and further childbearing in England and Wales. *Population Trends, 111*, 18–26.
Ross, C. E., & Mirowsky, J. (1999). Parental divorce, life-course disruption, and adult depression. *Journal of Marriage and the Family, 61*(4), 1034–1045.

Sakai, T., & Higuchi, Y. (2005). The life course of "freeters": Employment, marriage, childbirth. *The Japanese Journal of Labour Studies, 535*, 29–41. (in Japanese).

Sato, R., & Iwasawa, M. (2006). Contraceptive use and induced abortion in Japan: How is it so unique among the developed countries? *The Japanese Journal of Population, 4*(1), 33–54.

Schoen, R., Rogers, S. J., & Amato, P. R. (2006). Wives' employment and spouses' marital happiness assessing the direction of influence using longitudinal couple data. *Journal of Family Issues, 27*(4), 506–528.

Schoppa, L. J. (2006). *Race for the exits: The unraveling of Japan's system of social protection*. Ithaca, NY: Cornell University Press.

Schulze, H. J., & H. Tyrell. (2002). What happened to the European family in the 1980s? The polarization between the family and other forms of private life. In F.-X. Kaufman, A. Kuijsten, H.-J. Schulze, & K. P. Strohmeier (Eds.), *Family life and family policies in Europe* (vol. 2, pp. 69–119). New York: Oxford University Press.

Schwartz, C. R. (2010). Earnings inequality and the changing association between spouses' earnings. *American Journal of Sociology, 115*(5), 1524–1557.

Schwartz, C. R., & Mare, R. D. (2005). Trends in educational assortative marriage from 1940 to 2003. *Demography, 42*(4), 621–646.

Shattuck, R. M., & Kreider, R. M. (2013). *Social and economic characteristics of currently unmarried women with a recent birth: 2011*. American Community Survey Reports. Washington, DC: US Census Bureau.

Shirahase, S., & Raymo, J. M. (2014). Single mothers and poverty in Japan: The role of intergenerational coresidence. *Social Forces, 93*(2), 545–569.

Shire, K. A. (2002). Stability and change in Japanese employment institutions: The case of temporary work. *Asien, 84*, 21–30.

Sigle-Rushton, W., & McLanahan, S. (2002). The living arrangements of new unmarried mothers. *Demography, 39*(3), 415–433.

Smith, J. R., Brooks-Gunn, J., & Klebanov, P. K. (1997). Consequences of living in poverty for young children's cognitive and verbal ability and early school achievement. In G. J. Duncan & J. Brooks-Gunn (Eds.) *Consequences of growing up poor* (pp. 132–189). New York: Russell Sage Foundation.

Smits, J., & Park, H. (2009). Five decades of educational assortative mating in 10 East Asian societies. *Social Forces, 88*(1), 227–255.

Smock, P. J., Manning, W. D., & Gupta, S. (1999). The effect of marriage and divorce on women's economic well-being. *American Sociological Review, 64*(6), 794–812.

Smock, P. J., Manning, W. D., & Porter, M. (2005). "Everything's there except money": How money shapes decisions to marry among cohabitors. *Journal of Marriage and Family, 67*(3), 680–696.

Sobotka, T. (2008). The diverse faces of the second demographic transition in Europe. *Demographic Research, 19*, 171–224.

Steiber, N., Berghammer, C., & Haas, B. (2015). Contextualizing the education effect on women's employment: A cross-national comparative analysis. *Journal of Marriage and Family, 78*(1), 246–261.

Stevenson, B., & Wolfers, J. (2007). *Marriage and divorce: Changes and their driving forces*. NBER Working Paper 12944, Cambridge, MA: National Bureau of Economic Research.

Sudo, N., Suzuki, M., & Yamada, T. (2012). *Inequalities in the Japanese economy during the lost decades*. CIRJE Working papers F-856. Center for International Research on the Japanese Economy, University of Tokyo.

Suzuki, T. (1991). Social Intermarriages in Japan. *Journal of Population Problems, 46*(4), 14–31. (in Japanese).

Sweeney, M. M. (2002). Two decades of family change: The shifting economic foundations of marriage. *American Sociological Review, 67*(1), 132–147.

Sweeney, M. M., & Cancian, M. (2004). The changing importance of white women's economic prospects for assortative mating. *Journal of Marriage and Family, 66*(4), 1015–1028.

Tach, L. (2015). Social mobility in an era of family instability and complexity. *The Annals of the American Academy of Political and Social Science, 657*(1), 83–96.

Tach, L., Edin, K., & McLanahan, S. (2011). *Multiple partners and multiple partner fertility in fragile families.* Center for Research on Child Wellbeing Working Paper No. WP11-10-FF. Princeton, NJ: Princeton University.

Thomson, E., Hanson, T. L., & McLanahan, S. S. (1994). Family structure and child well-being: Economic resources vs. parental behaviors. *Social Forces, 73*(1), 221–242.

Thomson, E., Lappegaard, T., Carlson, M., Evans, A., & Gray, E. (2014). Childbearing across partnerships in Australia, the United States, Norway, and Sweden. *Demography, 51*(2), 485–508.

Thomson, E., McLanahan, S. S., & Curtin, R. B. (1992). Family structure, gender, and parental socialization. *Journal of Marriage and the Family, 54*(2), 368–378.

Trostel, P., Walker, I., & Woolley, P. (2002). Estimates of the economic return to schooling for 28 countries. *Labour Economics, 9*(1), 1–16.

Tsuya, N. O., Bumpass, L. L., Choe, M. K., & Rindfuss, R. R. (2005). Is the gender division of labour changing in Japan? *Asian Population Studies, 1*(1), 47–67.

Tsuya, N. O., & Mason, K. O. (1995). Changing gender roles and below-replacement fertility in Japan. In K. O. Mason & A.-M. Jensen (Eds.), *Gender and family change in industrialized countries* (pp. 139–167). Oxford, UK: Clarendon Press.

Upchurch, D. M., Lillard, L. A., & Panis, C. W. (2002). Nonmarital childbearing: Influences of education, marriage, and fertility. *Demography, 39*(2), 311–329.

Van de Kaa, D. J. (1987). Europe's second demographic transition. *Population Bulletin, 42*, 1–59.

Van de Kaa, D. J. (2001). Second demographic transition. In N. J. Smelser & P. B. Baltes (Eds.), *The International encyclopedia of social and behavioral sciences* (2nd ed., pp. 3486–3488). Oxford, UK: Elsevier.

Ventura, S. J., & Bachrach, C. A. (2000). Nonmarital childbearing in the United States, 1940-99. *National Vital Statistics Reports, 48*(16).

Vespa, J., Lewis, J. M., & Kreider, R. M. (2013). *America's families and living arrangements: 2012. Current Population Reports*, P20–570. Washington, DC: U.S. Census Bureau.

Waldfogel, J., Craigie, T.-A., & Brooks-Gunn, J. (2010). Fragile families and child wellbeing. *The Future of Children, 20*(2), 87–112.

Watanabe, H., & Kondō, H. (1990). Marriage and class formation. In H. Okamoto & M. Naoi (Eds.), *Class structure in modern Japan 4: Women and class structure* (pp. 91–118). Tokyo: Tokyo Daigaku Shuppankai. (in Japanese).

Western, B., Bloome, D., & Percheski, C. (2008). Inequality among American families with children, 1975 to 2005. *American Sociological Review, 73*(6), 903–920.

World Economic Forum. (2014). *The global gender gap report.* http://reports.weforum.org/global-gender-gap-report-2014/

Wu, L. L. (1996). Effects of family instability, income, and income instability on the risk of a premarital birth. *American Sociological Review, 61*(3), 386–406.

Wu, L. L., & Martinson, B. C. (1993). Family structure and the risk of a premarital birth. *American Sociological Review, 58*(2), 210–232.

Yamaguchi, K. (2005). The declining fertility rate at the below replacement level: Determinants and countermeasures—the roles of husbands, workplaces, the government, and society. *Japanese Journal of Household Economics, 66*, 57–67. (in Japanese).

Yasuda, S. (1971). *Research on social mobility.* Tokyo: Tokyo Daigaku Shuppankai. (in Japanese).

Yu, W.-H. (2002). Jobs for mothers: Married women's labor force reentry and part-time, temporary employment in Japan. *Sociological Forum, 17*(3), 493–523.

Yu, W.-H. (2012). Better off jobless? Scarring effects of contingent employment in Japan. *Social Forces, 90*(3), 735–768.

Yu, W.-H. (2009). *Gendered trajectories: Women, work, and social change in Japan and Taiwan*. Stanford CA: Stanford University Press.

Zhou, Y. (2014). *Single mothers' in Japan: Attempts to balance work-care and exit poverty*. Tokyo: Japan Institute for Labour Policy and Training. (in Japanese).

The manufacturer's authorised representative in the EU is Springer Nature Customer Service Centre GmbH, Europaplatz 3, 69115 Heidelberg, Germany. If you have any concerns regarding our products, please contact ProductSafety@springernature.com

Printed and bound by CPI Group (UK) Ltd, Croydon, CR0 4YY
22/09/2026
02220981-0016